The Academic
Intrapreneur

The Academic Intrapreneur

STRATEGY, INNOVATION, AND MANAGEMENT IN HIGHER EDUCATION

Baron Perlman,
James Gueths,
&
Donald A. Weber

PRAEGER

New York
Westport, Connecticut
London

Library of Congress Cataloging-in-Publication Data

Perlman, Baron, 1946–
    The academic intrapreneur : strategy, innovation, and management in higher education / Baron Perlman, James Gueths, and Donald A. Weber.
        p. cm.
    Bibliography: p.
    Includes index.
    ISBN 0-275-92951-5 (alk. paper)
    1. Universities and colleges—United States—Administration.
2. Universities and colleges—United States—Planning. 3. Strategic planning—United States. I. Gueths, James. II. Weber, Donald A.
III. Title. IV. Title: Academic intrapreneur.
LB2341.P435   1988
378.73—dc19   88-6609

Library of Congress Catalog Card Number: 88-6609

ISBN: 0-275-92951-5

First published in 1988

Praeger Publishers, One Madison Avenue, New York, NY 10010
A division of Greenwood Press, Inc.

Printed in the United States of America

The paper used in this book complies with the
Permanent Paper Standard issued by the National
Information Standards Organization (Z39.48-1984).

10 9 8 7 6 5 4 3 2 1

ERRATUM

Unfortunately, an error appears on page 183. The final line of the page should have been printed as the first line. The corrected paragraph, beginning on page 182, should read:

We also believe that the enabling mechanisms of a Transpreneurial or Intrapreneurial Organization are best retained and strengthened through "practice" on real problems. The muscles of a sleeping giant soon grow soft. The expert culture needs problems worthy of an expert community's attention.

Contents

Table and Figures

Preface and Acknowledgments

Higher education is integral to our society's existence, achievements, development, and standard of living. Its colleges and universities are the envy of the world, while at the same time they are chastised repeatedly for not performing as well as they should. For colleges and universities must be managed well; they are not an ornament nor luxury in our world. "They are . . . main pillars of a modern society, load-bearing members of the main structure . . . " (Drucker, 1973, p. 44). As such, they are a major expense in a modern society, both in tax dollars and as a place where people spend their time and energy. Most importantly, these institutions embody our society's values, shape them, study them, understand them, and help them to be passed down from generation to generation. Academe is our future.

Like private-sector organizations, colleges and universities face complicated environments and troubled times; but, unlike businesses and corporations, colleges and universities seldom merge, seldom are acquired, and seldom (unless private) go out of business. How then are they to maintain their strengths and plan and build for a vital future for themselves and for us? The answer lies in striving to become alive, flexible, strong organizations. One means to this end lies in the process of intrapreneurship. In intrapreneurship, employees of a college or university are a prime source of ideas and their analysis and implementation. Intrapreneurship is a process by which large organizations use their own members to originate and implement new ventures and products. In other words, they use their good thinkers and good doers to ensure institutional strength. Through the use of intrapreneurial teams, institutions of higher education can solidify that which already works well, do away with that which is nonproductive, and implement new programs and ideas to better serve each institution's multiple constituencies.

Examples of intrapreneurial work are rare, not only for academic institutions but for organizations of any kind. It is the purpose of this book to delineate the importance, process, and understanding of intrapreneurship in academe. "Truth is impossible—and therein lies a truth" (Kanter, 1983a, p. 282). Organizations have differences in structure, in process, and in people; there is no "one way." Our description and understanding of intrapreneurship at our University provides one such view of "truth."

THE BOOK

The book has six parts. Part I has two chapters which provide an *Overview* and foundation for what follows. Chapter 1 discusses intrapreneurship in academe. Chapter 2 addresses the process of intrapreneurship and the person who is the intrapreneur.

Part II provides an understanding of *The Intrapreneur's World*. Chapter 3 focuses on leadership and with it vision, mission, trust, and integrity. Chapter 4 is a discussion of people and their empowerment. Chapter 5 provides an understanding of culture in organizations. Chapter 6 describes organizational system variables relevant to intrapreneurship (rewards, technology, value, bureacracy, structure, and strategic types).

Part III of the book moves to a different way of knowing intrapreneurship. It is here that we focus on *The Doing* through an exploration of an extensive fourteen-year-old intrapreneurial effort at our University. We use this example because it represents intrapreneurship in its entirety. It allows us to provide sufficient detail, which can serve to help academic intrapreneurs in their work while at the same time assisting other readers to ask questions about implications for their institutions of higher education, or any organization for that matter. The effort at our campus involved dramatic shifts of power, influence, and day-to-day behavior. Chapter 7 looks at the beginning, the place of history, and the past of our University. Chapter 8 looks at the intrapreneurial effort as it developed and was implemented.

In Part IV we take the language and ideas already presented and apply them to *Understanding* intrapreneurship. Specifically, in Chapter 9 we attempt to understand our University before and during the intrapreneurial changes. We use a model of the intrapreneurial process to assist in this understanding. Because of their importance, technology and culture are treated in separate chapters, 10 and 11. In Chapter 12 we present our wisdom, a discussion of the most important lessons we learned throughout the intrapreneurship and management of its products. It is here that we address how one keeps intrapreneurial projects "stuck," a change which becomes part of the fabric of an organization.

In Part V we look to the future. Chapter 13 describes a new type of organization, the *Transpreneurial Organization*, which embodies many of the percepts and concepts of intrapreneurship without necessarily vigorously emphasizing the change process. The Transpreneurial institution is one which values people and their empowerment and searches for internal strength and a future vitality. Chapter 14 focuses on the place of intrapreneurship within academe in the future.

In Part VI we provide an epilogue. In Chapter 15, the *Epilogue*, we provide information on the intrapreneurial products and their success and failure during the ten years subsequent to the intrapreneurship. This chapter provides a relatively long-term time perspective on the intrapreneurial process as well as a summing up on what took place at our University.

The book serves several purposes. If the reader pauses to question, agree or disagree, take notes, and think about what we have to say, then our efforts will not have been in vain. There is more than enough room, in academia or any industry, for issues of effectiveness, that is, asking the right questions. Other readers may take ideas and apply them in their own organizations. This is the only way things will change. Some readers may use the book to assist them in conceptualizing new or ongoing intrapreneurial work in their institutions or organizations. This may help improve chances of successful intrapreneurship. For another group of readers, the book may be helpful as they study intrapreneurship and especially, we hope, intrapreneurship in service organizations. Of the many purposes of the book, we value all.

There are many people we must acknowledge. The road to a formal statement about intrapreneurship has been a long one. A special debt of gratitude is owed to Jeffrey Cornwall for his insight, passion for ideas, and clarity in thinking. There are others who assisted in conceptualization and in finding correct facts to whom we are grateful: E. Alan Hartman, Susan Mc-Fadden, Marvin Mengeling, Michael Mussen, and Cliff Wood at Oshkosh, Robert Birnbaum at Columbia University, and Jack Wakeley at Western Carolina University. Still others offered moral support, sound advice, and technical assistance; they include Paul Ansfield, Lynn Grancorbitz, Marlene Herzing, Robert Lane, Larry Lang, Gloria Splittgerber, and Linda Wojahn. We thank everyone who gave generously of their time and opinions.

Last, we are grateful to our wives, Sandy, Shiela, and Judy, who allowed us to give attention, time, and affect to this book, some of which would have normally been focused on them. And to our children, whose attention and caring continued, "thanks."

PART I

OVERVIEW

Chapter 1
Intrapreneurship in Academe

Intrapreneurship is entrepreneurship turned inward; it is the new venture within an organization. *Entrepreneurship* is the American dream. It is the vision of someone with a quality idea who, passionately committed to its realization and usually working alone, develops the product or idea, pursues venture capital, sets up production, starts small, and builds. Entrepreneurship is done without an organization. Recently cited examples include Chemlawn, Nike, or Federal Express (Nayak and Ketteringham, 1986). But large organizations do not want to lose good people every time they have an idea in which they believe deeply. Such organizations need ways to develop new products from *within* the corporation. How else would 3M have produced and marketed little pieces of self-sticky paper or Sony trimphed with its Walkman or Toyota become the world leader in quality production of automobiles (Nayak and Ketteringham, 1986)?

Intrapreneurship allows corporations to hold on to their best innovators. It is a process by which people bring to reality and fruition their ideas (whether they are products or projects) within complex bureaucracies; this is where the job gets done. Intrapreneurship is the new conceptualization of innovation or organizational change. It is also the only way to attain many organizational goals; the only way we can say: "We have met the future successfully!" It is something we need a lot more of in academe.

This book is about intrapreneurship in academe. Our thesis is that corporate lessons of survival, competition, and success from an intrapreneurial perspective are relevant to institutions of higher education (and to any organization which needs to look to the future with some aliveness). We write about improving the productive capacity of a university.

The current literature describing corporations, organizations, and institutions marks an important transition in understanding organizational functioning. The new perspectives on leadership, excellence, and survival are so extensively different from what has gone before that they come close to representing a Kuhnian revolution in the scientific sense (Kuhn, 1970). Drucker (1988) heralds "The Coming of The New Organization." Peters and Waterman (1982) talk about the new organizational theory and functioning as abruptly and radically different from the prevailing wisdom and thinking. Kanter (1983a) talks about ". . . a critical watershed because they [American corporations] face a transforming economic and social environment . . . " (p. 35). Gee and Tyler (1976) describe major changes affecting social and political environments.

Perspectives and understanding of corporations have been turned topsy-turvy. We view intrapreneurship in higher education from these *new* perspectives. Drucker (1985a) sees three parts to innovation and entrepreneurial work: strategy, innovation, and management. We will discuss these three elements in our case history of a successful intrapreneurial project offered as an example of what is possible in higher education.

This book focuses on the value of corporate lessons for academia. The academic messages (higher education literature) somehow do not capture the essence or spirit (Keller, 1983, is an exception) of changes needed to help colleges and universities survive and thrive. Business literature, when placed in juxtaposition to the academic literature, has passion, affect, and rhythm. Perhaps academic writing reflects the management climate of many institutions of higher education: a dry traditionalism. There is a fervor being preached in the private sector which is worth heeding.

The book is an outgrowth of our conceptualizations of a four-teen-year-old intrapreneurial effort at our University. The effort involved "revitalizing" the institution with a new academic calendar, a newly empowered faculty via a faculty development program, new patterns and uses of professional time, and other initiatives. In looking back, we wanted to understand what we had lived through and contributed to. "What did we really do?" we asked. "What are the implications of what we have done for solving the problems which face higher education and business alike?" "How have we come so far so quickly?" "Can culture be changed?" "Does an intrapreneurial academic institution make sense?" Some of the questions we pose contain part of the answers at which we arrived. We have moved beyond thinking in the academic language of our unique organizational setting to the language of culture, intrapreneurship, empowerment, technology, and positioning for the future.

For example, as we began to understand and interpret our University as an organization, and to apply corporate lessons and models to our experience, it became clear that this is a book about culture, power, and leadership. Its message is one of taking responsibility for problems, clearing the decks, and day by day helping move a university to where it needs to be. Higher education is entering a new era with new rules and new assumptions in which past management practices are inadequate to meet future challenges.

The Carnegie Commission on Higher Education in 1975 (*More Than Survival*) was arguing for better data, greater efficiency, greater effectiveness, quality, greater innovation, new culture (new assumptions), and institutional action. These were related to a series of important goals for higher education: strategic planning, flexibility, institutional specialization (finding a niche), increasing competitiveness, and becoming more autonomous. The Foundation called for new institutional missions, institutional identity, placing the burden on defending the status quo, quality ideas and innovative methods of implementing them, analysis, leadership, and imagination. Despite the grave dangers to higher education present in 1975, the report saw this as a time of opportunity.

The critical point made was that higher education could not

afford to wait for public policy to bail it out; there was no guarantee such a rescue would happen. Changes were needed; higher education had to avoid hubris and a false sense of its future security.

Had the Carnegie Foundation message for internal change, responsibility, and opportunity been acted on, colleges and universities might be better off today. The problems facing higher education have proved to be neither transitory nor minor: more economic difficulties; athletic scandals that highlight confusion over the place of academics in colleges and universities; confusion of roles, goals, and missions of educational institutions; competition from home and abroad. Even the quality, direction, and vitality of undergraduate education (Boyer, 1987) have been called into question.

Public policy has not bailed out higher education in the subsequent decade and may never do so. Academic organizations must themselves initiate changes to meet the stresses and pressures they face if they are to survive in a vital fashion. Higher education must be accountable to an agenda of goals and initiatives it sets for itself. The 1975 Carnegie Report did not articulate this vision in detail. Business literature and our own experiences now provide the expertise for making a well-formulated, clear expression of a vital academe in the future.

An equivalent state of events is taking place in business. Foreign competition, an increasingly complex environment, and changing consumer habits all serve to create a private-sector business climate of new assumptions. In the corporate literature, author after author argues for flexibility, a new sense of mission, identity, self-analysis, coherent strategy, and greater productivity.

But how do colleges and universities achieve these things? How do they reach for vitality? Where do they get ideas, experience, and wisdom? Where do they find people who have had success managing and solving difficult problems from an intrapreneurial perspective? They must listen to and seek out their own intrapreneurs.

There is a great demand for public institutions to become more innovative and dynamic (Ramamurti, 1986). Intrapreneurship must be applied to large institutions. The public expects that leaders of public institutions, just as for corporations, will identify opportunities that others do not see and be willing to take risks. "Risk, courage, individualism, innovation—without these, public institutions will fail. Eventually, politicians will stop voting to pay for them" (Kaplan, 1987, p. 89). The intrapreneurial discussion is a discussion of what higher education must be.

Why do colleges and universities have so few real leaders? Why are so few contemporary academic administrators known as heroes? Where is the intrapreneurial climate? Where are the intrapreneurs? When do we take control of our own destinies? Can this be done?

Higher education must differentiate between short-term and long-term issues. It must first determine and then place in priority order those problems which are institution wide, and those which most belong to the faculty, management, and students. It must ensure that solutions to short-term concerns do not have negative spill-over in the long run. The obverse of this is equally true. Solutions to long-term problems may have certain negative outcomes in the short run. Are colleges and universities willing to take risks? Can they tolerate ambiguity? Can the job get done? The good old days are now. It is time to make the best of them.

ACADEMIA AND INTRAPRENEURSHIP

There is little that is written for the intrapreneur working in any type of organization, especially colleges and universities. At the most basic level we know that service institutions are manageable only because some seem successful. If they are manageable they are capable of culture, structure, technology, and people who act as intrapreneurs. Most of the writing about service institutions we have found instructive is by Drucker (1973, 1985a). Drucker believes—this is the theme of our book—that universities need to be intrapreneurial and innovative fully as much as any business does. "Indeed they may need it more. The rapid changes in today's society, technology, and economy are simultaneously an even greater threat to them and an even greater opportunity" (Drucker, 1985a, p. 177).

Colleges and universities, whether public or private, have their idiosyncracies. They have multiple constituencies; legislators or other politicians often determine budgets, and, of course, universities have a unique decision-making process. This decision structure is complicated; on top of usual decision-making levels is a second pyramid called "governance." It is a curious marriage! Administrators control the purse, faculty control academic policy. Such institutions are dominated by bureaucratic rules but also by strong currents of collegiality and democracy. All three norms (democratic/political, bureaucratic, and collegial) must be understood by the intrapreneur.

Universities also may have more subgroups than many organizations their size. Cohen and March (1974) call them organized anarchies. " . . . common concerns over parking space and central heating are all that bind universities together . . . " (Lindquist, 1978, p. 23). The statement may be harsh but it has a ring of truth. Universities often have little sense of common community.

But a college or university is no more difficult an organization in which to institute intrapreneurial projects or programs than any other corporation or institution. Changing the status quo may be difficult, but it is not impossible. We agree with Drucker's (1985a) contention that most innovations are probably driven by outsiders or catastrophe. But we cannot bemoan academe's loss of autonomy if we are unwilling to take the rudder and try to pilot the course of our institutions ourselves.

Intrapreneurship is possible in university settings, but intrapreneurs must know their organizations well. For example, academic institutions are not businesses (Drucker, 1973). Businesses focus on results; service institutions tend to focus on efficiency, not effectiveness. By this we mean they are more prone to worry about and emphasize doing things right (efficiency) than doing the right things. Even this emphasis on efficiency must be interpreted in the narrow sense of the term. Many service organizations try to get as many resources as they can and they spend as much as they get. What is needed are effective *and* efficient institutions of higher education. If this goal is realized, then Lindquist's (1978) observation might no longer be valid that universities are places for all sorts of new ideas, great places to get new ideas initiated, but terrible places to get them implemented.

A second problem the intrapreneur must confront is the fact that many people who work in colleges and universities tend to be frustrated and focused on red tape and procedure, not on performance and results. Higher education has enough good people. Intrapreneurship would be easier and more prevalent if time and energy could be focused on results, not on bureaucratic barriers to organizational quality, change, and renewal.

Third, colleges and universities have "intangible objectives." Although business' objectives are not that tangible either, businesses are able to translate their statements into operational, quantitative terms; institutions of higher education do not. "[T]he starting point for effective work is a definition of the purpose and mission of the institution—which is almost always 'intangible' but nevertheless need not be vacuous" (Drucker, 1973, p. 49).

For service institutions, success is defined by a larger budget; for business, it is results. Businesses are paid for satisfying customers, public-sector colleges and universitites are paid because they exist. Because public academic institutions are paid out of a budget allocation, their revenue is tied to a tax, not necessarily to performance. Qualitative failure often does not lead, at least in the near term, to budget reductions. And when successes occur there is no guarantee that larger budgets will accrue! This focus on budget (and politics), not performance (customers or opportunity), as Drucker points out, deceives the public and ourselves. The end result is often ineffectiveness and inefficiency in service institutions. Taking a long-term view under these (fiscal) circumstances is frustrating and commands creative work.

All colleges and universities are dependent on a multitude of constituents, each important and each with different priorities. How does an organization set priorities, cut nonproductive programs, and concentrate its efforts when it must please everyone? "[B]eing budget-based makes it even more difficult to abandon the wrong things, the old, the obsolete. As a result, service institutions are even more encrusted than businesses with the barnacles of inherently unproductive efforts" (Drucker,

1973, p. 52). How correct Drucker is. He further argues (1973) that nothing is ever accomplished unless " . . . scarce resources are concentrated on a small number of priorities" (p. 52). Is it any wonder education, especially public education, is having problems? Doing a little bit of everything really means achieving nothing.

Public universities are rewarded for what society deems they deserve rather than for what they earn. They are paid for good intentions and for programs, not for successes. Important constituencies must not be alienated.

Colleges and universities exist to meet society's needs. But their social responsibility is not necessarily greater than that of private-sector corporations. Both have moral commitments. But the mission of higher education is defined in a more absolute moral sense (rather than being subject to cost/benefit analysis and change strategies), which increases the probability of institutional stagnation. In this milieu of moral imperatives, if moral goals are not met colleges and universities almost always redouble their efforts to meet the moral needs of society and its members. As a result, precious resources are allocated with few positive outcomes possible. What often results is a waste of time, money, and people.

Stated another way, colleges and universities are maximizing organizations, not optimizing ones. The closer they come to their objectives, the harder they work on what they are already doing (maximizing). An alternative strategy would be to put these additional resources into new and developing programs and areas in which there would be a much greater return on investment (optimizing).

In maximizing institutions, intrapreneurship or change is usually perceived as an attack on the organization's commitment, its beliefs, and its values. Such organizations, as is true of many colleges and universities, never cut bait; they fish on forever.

Drucker (1973) states that universities need to engage in some very basic organizational behaviors in order to be more intrapreneurial. First, missions must be clearly defined. Colleges and universities need effectiveness; in other words, higher education must move beyond empty rhetoric. Why does our regional university exist? Do our programs exist to meet our mission and goals? Does the past have to drive the future?

Second, such organizations need a realistic statement of goals. If colleges and universities are to be open to change, they must have some sense of direction. With a sense of direction for the future, positive movement may occur in the organization, which allows for the eventual enumeration of more specific institutional objectives.

Last, they must have policies and practices which allow a search for innovation and opportunity. The "Search for Opportunity" is what we believe intrapreneurship is all about in academic institutions.

Colleges and universities must pay greater attention to quality and effectiveness issues. If society gets Pablum in the disguise of good education, institutions of higher education will suffer the consequences. The stakes are high.

Colleges and universities are too important to be traditional in all their segments. It is possible that institutions of higher education are stuck on the wrong things. Maintaining the place of society's past and tradition is one of their strengths; but making organizational structure and practices a tradition in and of themselves is madness. Competition will come from somewhere, either from other colleges and universities, from the private sector, or from our customers themselves. Perhaps in years to come historians will look back and point to the traditionalism of colleges and universities as a major failure leading to our society's stagnation or decline.

OUR PURPOSE: INTRAPRENEURSHIP IN ACADEME

The purpose of this book is to provide an understanding of intrapreneurs and intrapreneurship applicable to academic institutions. We are writing about getting things done. It is that simple and that complex. We look especially at intrapreneurship as it involves management, faculty, and support staff. We will leave for other authors the application of intrapreneurship in all its richness and subtlety to other strategy makers, state system administrators, or elected political officials.

In essence, we are writing about the internal life of an organization. Ultimately each campus is responsible for what it is, what it becomes, and how it manages its present and future. Intrapreneurship is a way by which many academic organizations and their faculties can claim or reclaim an excitement and dynamism which they have never had or have lost.

Intrapreneurship as a process encapsulates much of what is needed in academia. If strategic planning as an outgrowth of incrementalist and rational planning models is as important to academia as Keller (1983) believes it is, then intrapreneurship must be equally distinguished as a process, for it is by this method that such planning will be implemented.

The intrapreneurial process emphasizes integrity; people must be treated with respect. There is great emphasis on people's autonomy and responsibility within organizations. There also must be solid thinking about questions and their answers, problems and their solutions. Quality and value are necessary; colleges and universities cannot sell out for student credit hours or image; they need *real* programs and a hard-earned reputation.

Quality of organizational life, leadership, rewards, recognition, opportunity, use of power, trust, technology—intrapreneurship can use these to alleviate many of the problems confronting higher education. For those readers who work in state systems, intrapreneurship is a powerful tool with which to counteract the "crunch" that occurs when states cut funds for higher education, or when we find our state schools under tighter state control.

Either we give up and say that the forces (internal and external) buffeting higher education are too great and too complex and admit we are not up to the task, or we let some people who are up to the task get something done. Our future is in our own hands (Carnegie Council, 1980). And if our intrapreneurial projects do not all succeed (and they will not) at least we will live our academic days fighting for a better academe, not acquiescing to a mediocre or average status quo.

Chapter 2
Intrapreneurship and the Intrapreneur

We are in the midst of a revolution. Our society is moving from an industrial framework and infrastructure to an informational one. Our economy is not national anymore; it is worldwide in scope. Decentralization seems to have more potential than centralization. Small is better and beautiful. Hierarchies are "out," networking is in. The world requires more social and organizational innovation.

Many new business ideas are markedly different from management theory which went before. One gives away power in order to get power. One loosens up in order to maintain controls. The group or team is more important than the individual. One looks for long-standing ghosts, images, and elders in the organization in order to understand the past to better know the present. One needs an organization with sages who have visions of the future. Throughout, a code of values and ethics, including integrity and trust, forms the roles for organizational work.

Another deviation from traditional wisdom involves the perception and treatment of time. If organizations are to survive, they can no longer avoid careful analysis of their environments nor of themselves. To accomplish this they must supplement information and knowledge of the here and now with a respect for, and the careful heed of, the future. We are asked to think beyond this fiscal year to five years or even ten years hence. Organizations must build toward long-term successes in small ways.

Affect has taken a prominent place in organizational success and failure. What becomes important are the feelings and perceptions individuals within an organization hold about its goals, ideas, how to behave, its future, their future, and having fun. Passion used to be called a lack of objectivity. Now it is called commitment (Pinchot, 1985). Rituals, stories, and heroes guide behavior; express the values of the corporation; and move us away from sole dependence on rationality.

The thinking of those influential in the business and organizational world has relevance to academia and, more specifically, to change and success in higher education. We must, therefore, take a closer look at intrapreneurship and the intrapreneur.

INTRAPRENEURSHIP

Compared to entrepreneurship, in which one goes into business for oneself, intrapreneurship involves serving oneself and the company or organization in which one works. Intrapreneurship is a process by which a person meets his or her needs for autonomy, invention, management, and completion of projects in a complex bureaucracy. It is a process by which new ventures, products, and projects are developed and implemented in large organizations. Intrapreneurship is one of the most important phenomena in American business today.

Peters and Austin (1985) view constant innovation as one of only three elements needed for organizational success. Foster (1986), without naming intrapreneurship per se, describes the process as the attackers' advantage as the world drives to make corporations and their products obsolete. Drucker (1985a) considers innovation and change as central to our enconomy. If resource problems occur, then existing resources must be utilized to compete, or the organization dies.

Intrapreneurship from this perspective is functional; it helps an organization adapt to a changing environment and to new needs in productive, life-giving ways. In describing twelve products and ideas which changed how we think and live in our world, Nayak and Ketteringham (1986) write about intrapreneurship. Lindquist (1978) is more sanguine but people's underlying interests, habits, fears, and prejudices are not serious problems, as long as an organization can be served by positive intrapreneurship.

Intrapreneurship is the way by which organizations position for a productive future. "The notion is at base a simple one. If all the organization's energy and skill is put into implementation of existing policies and programs, that is what the organization is going to do, even if the resulting status quo is not working" (Lindquist, 1978, p. 253). Intrapreneurship is the commitment of people within corporations and institutions to new ventures.

Kanter (1983a) defines change masters as those people and organizations adept at anticipating the need for, and of leading, productive change. Kanter's contention that intrapreneurshp does not need to stop in resources' lean times is particularly relevant to public universities today.

Kanter (1983a) writes, and our experiences support her, that an organization's structure, climate, and culture must allow people to play the "game." The critical reward is not money, which makes these "games" all the more applicable to public organizations where money is often in short supply. Involvement in constructive-change projects is a powerful and meaningful experience for organizational members. Being involved with internal organizational change brings with it role variety; it allows individuals to escape from the usual routine into something new. People work and interact with others in the organization with whom they normally do not spend time. They are allowed some risk taking and a chance of succeeding, of becoming heroes. Involvement allows visibility, recognition, a sense of belonging, and a feeling of commitment (Kanter, 1972). It allows those who want to contribute to the organization a chance to do so.

But most of all, it allows people to play the game! And the most positive outcome of participating is that the next time there is a game they may be chosen for the team. Intrapreneurship allows people to both work hard *and* have fun. It is a perfect organizational activity for those who take their games seriously.

Either organizations allow their people (good–best–all) intrapreneurial opportunities, or many will leave and become competitors or they will psychologically withdraw and contribute less. People in academe, as in other large organizations, need opportunity and power or they become "stuck" (Kanter, 1979). Organizations which have no room for intrapreneurship create negative climates because employees who are frustrated in attempts to implement good ideas can remain, become unproductive, or even fester.

Intrapreneurship is a team effort and as such it celebrates teams, not individual heroes. It is collective entrepreneurship. Intrapreneurship changes the way relationships are perceived and valued. Interdependence and contributions to the common good are celebrated. Many of the intrapreneurial success stories in the business literature point to a hero, only because they would be more difficult to write and probably less interesting if there was not a strong protagonist. But Reich (1987) is convincing that the mythical version of America with its entrepreneurial hero must be supplanted; it is obsolete. The group becomes greater than its individual members.

There are three classic images of the polity that clarify this issue. The first is the ship of state, which is one thing if it is to be forever at sea, and quite another if it is to reach port and the passengers go their separate ways. They think about one another and their relationships on the ship very differently in the two cases. The former case is the ancient city; the latter, the modern state. The other two images are the herd and the hive, which oppose each other. The herd may need a shepherd, but each of the animals is grazing for itself and can easily be separated from the herd. In the hive, by contrast, there are workers, drones and a queen: there is a division of labor and a product toward which they all work in common; separation from the hive is extinction. The herd is modern, the hive is ancient. (Bloom, 1987, pp. 112–113)

The hive or ancient city are metaphors for an organization which values intrapreneurship. The herd or modern state more accurately reflects our society's emphasis on the individual. It is the former of which we need more.

Intrapreneurship implies taking an idea and implementing it. Thus intrapreneurship has two critical dimensions. The first is good ideas, the second the ability and interest in making them real. Organizations maximize the former by keeping good people and allowing them opportunities to communicate and create good ideas. The latter, making ideas into reality—getting the job done—is complicated; it is what this book is about.

How does intrapreneurship come about? How can we understand the genesis of intrapreneurial ideas and how or if they are implemented?

There are two hypotheses for the genesis of intrapreneurial work. These are the big bang and incremental theories (Clifford and Cavanagh, 1985; Kanter, 1983a). Does intrapreneurship evolve slowly over time, simmering and cooking before ready for consumption? Does it follow the slow evolution of species model? Or does intrapreneurship evolve rapidly from nothingness; that is, the quicker, more immediate Big Bang theory of the universe? Or like light (both a wave and particles) does intrapreneurship (paradoxically) have its genesis in both?

More specifically, we do have some ideas about how intrapreneurship develops. There are unplanned change opportunities; the gift horse does come calling on occasion. There are crises which often mandate a "change or die" strategy. Some organizations have superstars, persons who by the strength of intellect, persistence, and motivation are able to get something new done. There are such people in academic settings. Kanter (1983a) talks about an interesting reason for change: the Lone Ranger or deviant/bureaucratic insurgent who, by taking advantage of loopholes, avoiding rules, evading formal orders, and just plain breaking the rules, gets something done.

Many colleges and universities have been struggling for some time with change, some successfully, some less so. This evolution and change in academic institutions must continue.

THE INTRAPRENEUR

The power of intrapreneurship as an idea and process is that it involves more than product lines; it is also intimately tied to retention of valued organizational members. In *Break-Throughs*, Nayak and Ketteringham (1986) describe common elements of intrapreneurship: emotion, loyalty, and people. All three components both create and retain good people. One needs good people who have good ideas and who also have a *passion* for these ideas (Pinchot, 1985). Whether gradual or sudden, change comes about because there are people (intrapreneurs) to solve organizational problems. It may sound simplistic, but it is true; change comes about because people do things. When all is said and done someone has to go out and do something. Someone has to get the job done as best he or she can (Lindquist, 1978).

Intrapreneurs are "dreamers who do." They exist at all levels in an organization. An intrapreneur is not an inventor per se, but one who takes responsibility for creating innovation *within* an organization. Intrapreneurs are dreamers in the sense that they figure out how to turn an idea into a profitable reality.

Intrapreneurs are people working for themselves within organizations, that is, people wanting and expecting to meet some of their own needs such as autonomy, responsibility, and ownership. Intrapreneurs thrive within an organizational structure which is not overly preoccupied with control and analysis but has room for new ideas, ambiguity, and change.

Intrapreneurs are concerned with issues such as "Opportunity," "How to capitalize on opportunity," "What resources are needed for an intrapreneurial effort?," "How is control gained over these resources?," and "What structure is best to allow positive change?"

In contrast, managers are concerned with issues such as "Stability" (not change), "What resources can be controlled?," "What structure determines the organization's relationship to its market?," "How can the impact of others on their ability to perform be minimized?," and "What opportunity is appropriate?" (Betz, 1987).

In a new or growing organization, intrapreneurs should predominate. In a mature organization, intrapreneurs and stewards should be properly balanced. Success comes from both effectiveness and efficiency. Intrapreneurs pay attention to vision, to newness; stewards pay attention to balance, organization, efficiency, and stable growth. Betz (1987) believes that an organization fails when either kind of leadership is missing.

We argue that management in colleges and universities is overbal-

anced toward the steward end of the continuum; we need more intra-preneurs. We also need to structure our academic organizations so that their intrapreneurs have a greater chance of success.

Intrapreneurs undertake difficult and complicated tasks; theirs is not an easy lot. Because of the complexities in their work, they fail for a multitude of reasons. They may work in organizations which have little or no use for intrapreneurship—recalcitrant bureaucracies. They may have poor interpersonal skills. They may ignore affect and climate and stick with rational, intellectual solutions. They may lack financial or technological skills. They may not appreciate the market or understand the customer. They may wear out under the rigors of always persevering. They may simply be unlucky.

There will always be opposition to intrapreneurial efforts. The quality and value of an idea never suffices in and of itself. Lindquist (1978) calls these omnipresent opponents "nibbling piranhas." Intrapreneurs need mechanisms to defeat and disarm opponents. Kanter (1983a) provides a shopping list of these mechanisms, including waiting them out, wearing them down, appealing to larger principles, inviting them in (if you can't beat them, have them join you), sending emissaries to smooth the way and plead your case, displaying support, reducing the stakes, and warning the critics. No wonder it is so hard to maintain enthusiasm throughout the life span of an intrapreneurial project! Regardless of resources and opportunity in an organization, there are numerous factions who want these resources. Nothing comes easily.

In the public organization, academia included, there are several barriers to intrapreneurship which people use as excuses against meaningful change (Ramamurti, 1986). The multiplicity and ambiguity of public organizations' goals is seen as paralyzing management. Limited managerial autonomy and the high potential for interference are seen as discouraging innovation and intrapreneurship. Being visible in the media is tied to overly cautious behavior. A skewed reward system is perceived as penalizing failures and mistakes but rarely in rewarding success. The short-term orientation of public organizations, we are told, discourages large innovative strategic change with long-term payoff.

Finally, restrictions on personnel practices may hinder finding the best people and rewarding them or in discharging nonproductive individuals, thereby reducing a leader's ability to motivate subordinates and implement programs.

Yet all of these barriers can be overcome; none need prevent successful intrapreneurial work. One does not, in a public organization, improve the probability of change occurring and its quality "by exhorting politicians and bureaucrats to provide managers clear goals, adequate autonomy, better incentives, and then to desist from 'interfering' in all but policy matters. This . . . seldom works in practice" (Ramamurti, 1986, p. 155). What does work is having good intrapreneurs.

Good intrapreneurs have team-building skills and the ability to lead. They want to see flowers bloom in the desert. They tolerate ambiguity, can make decisions (often without enough data), and they trust their feelings. They have courage. It is scary to take risks. Their strength is the ability to envision all the things which have to fall in place, all the landmines and pitfalls to be avoided, all the people (and when, who, and in what order and manner) to touch base with if the intrapreneurial idea is to become a reality. They imagine customers for their product. They are persistent and have dedication. They are obsessed with how to get a new idea to fruition. Simply put, they ask how they can get from Point A to Point B within their organizations.

The benefits of intrapreneurs in an organization are obvious. They introduce new products, processes, and services which enable the company to profit and grow. They can take a position which was initially powerless and unimportant and make it a base for intrapreneurship, that is, for serving the organization. Intrapreneurs are the hope for the future because things happen when people are passionately dedicated to making them happen.

It is interesting to look at what motivates and characterizes intrapreneurs. They are not driven by a desire for wealth. They use analytic skills in concert with their intuitive skills. They are not amoral. They are not power-hungry empire builders. They are instead motivated to get something done (this can be threatening in any organization where the status quo is valued). They try to anticipate barriers, remain open to feedback, and do not court risk (promoters court risk). Finally, they are honest with themselves and with others. As a matter of fact, Pinchot (1985) notes that their ability to detect malarkey is remarkable. Intrapreneurs search for opportunity.

Those who work in higher education are buffeted by rules, directives, and multiple constituencies. What has happened in public academe is that a complex set of procedures and rules has been built up. These rules serve to extend the notion of collegial decision-making to large organizations. But this collegium is tough to maintain within a large group, especially an academic organization composed largely of individuals committed to so much outside the institution (ideas, professional organizations, etc.). In a sense, academia has constructed a kind of procedure-bound legalistic system (some might consider it Pharisaic) that stifles the intrapreneur. It is difficult in a litigious academic organization to participate effectively in fast-moving change processes.

But academic intrapreneurs, if they are to positively assist their institutions, must step back from the maelstrom to look calmly at the entire academic organizational mosaic or collage. It is this detached observation of the whole which will assist academic intrapreneurs in their strivings to position their institutions for a vital future, to act on their own initiatives instead of reacting. Searching for opportunity is a breath of fresh air.

Kanter (1983a) describes change as opportunity or threat; intrapreneurs view it as the former. Intrapreneurs understand that the pain of change is useful, an exhilarating challenge, a means of cleaning house. Kanter is correct when she observes that change is exhilarating when done *by* us and disturbing when done *to* us. We need more "done by us" in higher education.

One analogy of opportunity (Drucker, 1985a) is that each type of opportunity is a window in a building, all facing different directions, each giving a small view of the outside. Pieced together they present a patchwork of opportunities; taken separately they provide distinct and different perceptions.

In summary, it is the bright idea, a person with an idea, that is the major and most important source of innovation and change. A person with an idea who wants to turn that idea into a program or product is an intrapreneur. Getting the bright idea adopted is the hard work.

We have only a limited number of maps to show us how to successfully negotiate the landmines which lie between idea, opportunity, and implementation. To make the complex simpler, Kanter (1983a) sees three major phases of intrapreneurial activity: problem definition, organizational business (building coalitions, blessings from the top, trading, cheerleading, etc.), and keeping the project going to completion. We would add a fourth phase; managing the completed project to ensure its future.

What intrapreneurs "do" never happens as planned; no one can accurately plan something that is really new. Intrapreneurs grope toward solutions. This is not to say they do not plan; they plan in great detail to minimize risk and maximize success. Obstacles (think of them as mines floating beneath the surface of the water, unseen but lurking dangerously) must be anticipated, and approaches to overcome them marked. Strategies must be developed to build on intrapreneurial successes.

Quinn (1985a) has captured the essence of intrapreneurship and what the intrapreneur faces day to day. "One should recognize and manage innovation as it really is—a tumultuous, somewhat random, interactive learning process linking a worldwide network of knowledge sources to the subtle unpredictability of customers' end uses (p. 6)."

The following chapters discuss four important dimensions in the intrapreneur's world. These are leadership, empowerment, culture, and organizational-level processes such as reward systems and bureaucracies.

PART II

THE INTRAPRENEUR'S WORLD

Chapter 3
Leadership

Leadership is a crucial part of the intrapreneur's world. Both an organization and an intrapreneurial team must have leadership. It is so important that Peters and Austin (1985) define leadership as one of the three elements of successful organizations. In a study of mid-size companies, Clifford and Cavanagh (1985) concluded that leadership at the top, the ability to orchestrate strategy and structure, and the leader's ability to instill and institutionalize vision emerge as the singular distinguishing characteristic of winning performance.

Leadership is the process by which organizational cultures are formed and changed. We like the metaphor of leadership as pathfinding, with implications for discovering new routes and new ways, and a comfort with ambiguity and the unknown.

We must have leaders because they solve problems. They cut through complicated environments both inside and outside of organizations. In one sense they simplify the complex. It is their vision of the future and the meanings they communicate which provide a framework for decision-making and interpreting the complex day-to-day world in which people work.

Leaders must focus on asking the correct questions and on providing alternate scenarios of what most people view as a fixed reality. This framework, which Schein (1985a) conceptualizes as organizational culture, is a set of filters or lenses that help people who work or live in large organizations to focus on and perceive relevant portions of their environment. There can be no solutions without new assumptions (Kanter, . 1983a).

In other words, "managers do things right, leaders do the right things" (Bennis and Nanus, 1985). Managers are concerned with efficiency, leaders with effectiveness.

VISION

Organizations need leaders with vision. Vision implies asking what an institution might become. Vision is the bricks and mortar which makes dreams come true, but it is also affect and perceptions. People must believe. They must believe that what they do is important; they must believe that their organization is moving toward a better tomorrow; they must believe that today will be meaningful and perhaps fun—that they can make a contribution, and that others know they have done so. "When you identify with your company's purpose, when you experience ownership in a shared vision, you find yourself doing your life's work instead of just doing time" (Naisbitt and Aburdene, 1985, p. 26).

The importance of vision is that intrapreneurial efforts, given the ambiguity and stresses they create within organizations, must contribute to the goals and mission of that organization. Vision is the avenue by which organizations reach their potential. Otherwise why engage in all that risky behavior and hard work? It is vision which gives people a sense of what might be, not pie in the sky what might be, but a realistic articulation of a future image.

Vision is the road down which intrapreneurs drive. This road provides the straightest route from idea to concrete reality. Intrapreneurial efforts translate ideas into reality; visions provide an infrastructure for the process. Visions are the blueprints which guide construction of intrapreneurial products and projects. It is these outcomes of the intrapreneurs' work which form a bridge between the present technology and ways of doing things in the future.

To succeed, visions must be effective. While it is usually the corporate executive who forges the vision, intrapreneurs in an organization can contribute to the vision and, if open communication exists, can share their own visions of what the organization might become.

In other words, leaders define the reality of their organizations. This seems like grand work, uplifting stuff of which to be a part. What it is really is extremely hard work! In defining the mission, the vision, and the meaning of their organizations, leaders have to stick to a singular definition of reality. They have to be able to show how this reality encompasses the environment (customers and purchase of products or services), the present, the future, and the people who work in the organization. And leaders had better love the reality they are defining because they are stuck with it day after day. Persistence in the pursuit of a singular vision is hard labor.

There are limits to what any college or university can or would want to become. Visions must be tied to the doable and reachable. "The university must resist the temptation to try to do everything for society. The university is only one interest among many and must always keep its eye on that interest for fear of compromising it in the desire to be more useful, more relevant, more popular" (Bloom, 1987, p. 254).

For many academic institutions, questions of reality, mission, and "who we are" go unanswered. The vision is muddled.

A MISSION

Good leadership with vision provides a corporation or institution with an important asset—its mission. Successful organizations have an evangelical sense of mission. A mission is what Moses brings down from the mountain for the people; it distills the articles of faith. Yet college and university "mission statements are traditionally innocent pieces of fiction . . . " (Jellema, 1986, p. 8). The process of defining mission and vision is not transacted very often in colleges and universities (Keller, 1983). Writing from a strategic planning perspective, Keller argues for the importance of knowing "our places," knowing "who we really are," knowing "what we value most," knowing "what business we are really in," knowing "what is most central to us," and knowing "how to proceed." These are mission, effectiveness, and vision issues. Missions drive an organization's behavior for years to come. In academia the future is all around us but many of us cannot seem to find it.

TRUST AND INTEGRITY

Leaders overcome organizational complexities and clarify organizational ambiguity. To do this they must possess credibility, integrity, and trust. If leaders do not behave in ethical and responsible ways in their interactions with others, they will not succeed. They must take care of and protect their people. Intrapreneurs, for example, are straight with people; they have to be. People are the most important resource in intrapreneurial work; good people are a precious resource. After all, new ideas are a red flag demanding an audit from organizational members. To pass these audits, the intrapreneur must have people's respect and trust.

Trust implies accountability, predictability, and reliability. Trust and integrity are not established in a vacuum. They come out of interactions and relationships which leaders establish with people in their organizations. Leaders are involved in many interactions and transactions. Leaders must have the time to attend not only to vision and meaning but to people. Leaders must not only be listened to, they must listen to others. This is very important.

"Trust is the glue that maintains organizational integrity" (Bennis and Nanus, 1985, p. 44); "Trust is the emotional glue that binds followers and leaders together" (Bennis and Nanus, 1985, p. 153). Trust cannot be purchased nor are there any shortcuts to its establishment and maintenance. It must be earned. Organizational leaders and intrapreneurs (who lead intrapreneurial teams) set a climate or culture for ethics, integrity, and trust in the ways they behave and their commitment to these values.

Credibility is power plus competence (Kanter, 1983b). Leaders need more than the ability to command resources, information, or legitimacy. Once these are available, they need the ability to deliver a "product" as promised. Keeping promises is a matter of personal integrity; it engenders trust. Positioning people in an organization so that power is available will not result in leadership if they lack the abilities to use power well. Equally true, people with abilities to lead cannot lead easily or well without power. Both commodities are needed for credibility.

INTRAPRENEURIAL LEADERSHIP

Each intrapreneurial team has a leader, analogous to the organization's chief executive officer. Each new venture—intrapreneurial project—has its own environment, both external to and internal to the organization as a whole. Each intrapreneurial team is attempting to maintain a positive climate, to empower its members, and reward them. It may have a culture congruent with or different from an organizationwide one (an organization can have multiple cultures). Each group needs leadership and with it vision, strategy, and meaning.

Intrapreneurs must set the direction for their teams. Just as the chief executive officer attempts to give people vision, meaning, and a sense of community or belonging, so, too, the intrapreneurial leader wants individuals to feel good about their contributions, to celebrate good news, to build rituals, to have fun, to listen to and respect others, and to be committed to the task and group at hand. It is the intrapreneurial leader who must focus on what is being built. Thus, the intrapreneurial leader must be comfortable working alone, planning, thinking, and defining, and must be comfortable with others in networking, team building, begging, pleading, and presenting.

Intrapreneurs face many "dilemmas of teamwork" (Kanter, 1983a) which leadership can help overcome. For example, people on an intrapreneurial team may be loathe to "cross" a higher-up, or speak frankly to him or her. People on the intrapreneurial team may have to be taught how to participate. Members of the team have different skills which have to be blended and tossed together like a salad. Selection of team members is important (the most important decisions involve people and who will participate); avoid know-it-alls and cliques. Hidden agendas have to be avoided; they have no place in intrapreneurial work. Team politics must be dealt with and squashed. The intrapreneurial leader has neither the time nor the energy for them. Issues of toes (getting stepped on) and hands (getting slapped) must be attended to. There are issues of NIH (not invented here) mentalities, ownership, and egos.

And one must be aware that intrapreneurial work has its own rhythm and pace. There are times to goad people to work hard and times to let them coalesce, think, philosophize, and then work hard again. The intrapreneurial leader has to be sensitive to all this. Intrapreneurial team leaders are like orchestra conductors (except that a complete score telling where they are going and how the project will end is not available. Intrapreneurship is a perennial unfinished symphony.). One cues in and cues out various players, decides how loud or soft they will play, decides the pace or tempo, and must deal with the players' personalities.

Intrapreneurs as leaders must be both transforming (mentor, sponsor, value shaper, exemplar, maker of meanings, and/or pathfinder) and transactional (maintaining the coalition, culture, and present status of the project or new product).

We seem to have woefully few executives with intrapreneurial orientations in our colleges and universities and thus we need to look for intrapreneurs at all levels in a university. While leadership at the top of an organization is critically important, this is *not* the only place *leaders* can be found. The truth is that academic (and other) institutions need leadership at any and all organizational levels. While it is often the chief executive officer who, for better or worse, sets the tone and rhythm for the corporation, the leader of an intrapreneurial team is also empowered to wind the works and make the clock tick.

SUCCESSION

Leaders really have no allegiance to organizations. They honor their sponsors and their ideas but they will move on automatically once they have "rooted" these ideas in the organization. They will move on sooner if they are frustrated because they cannot implement these ideas. No leader is forever. Managers, on the other hand, honor organizations since they see their future within them. Thus, managers are likely to work longer in an organization than are leaders. Since we argue that leaders invariably move on, the issue of succession is an important one.

Succession is the process by which leadership is maintained. Clifford and Cavanagh (1985) write that, "Perhaps the wisdom and the skill to carry out effective transition are among the ultimate tests as to whether the winning company has truly achieved a lastingly effective organization" (p. 152). Good leadership implies having others waiting in the wings who can be successful and an organization with a strong enough climate and a clear enough mission that a search for a successor can be successfully accomplished.

Succession is equally important at the intrapreneurial team level. If a project is successful there must be people waiting who can take over and market, manage, and ensure its future. The intrapreneur must be willing to give way to someone else. One advantage intrapreneurs have is that the nature of their work forces them to cut across formal organizational communication and structural lines and allows them to become intimately aware of the talented people from whom to draw and choose a successor(s).

But leadership is not the entirety of the intrapreneur's world. Empowering others to be valuable and responsible organizational members is equally important. It is to the concept of empowerment that we now turn.

Chapter 4
People and Their Empowerment

"Powerlessness corrupts. Absolute powerlessness corrupts absolutely" (Kanter, 1983b, p. 258). People must not feel condescended to. "You don't give someone opportunity as though it were a gift. You present them with a chance and hope like hell they grab it" (Kanter, 1983a, p. 246).

A popular vision today for leaders involves the concept of empowerment: giving others in the organization the power to get work done. The idea and process of empowerment also includes exercising power to remove barriers for the empowered. More and more leaders realize that, to have an effective and efficient organization, its members must be given autonomy (in the past "control" was kept at the top of an organization).

This vision of empowerment is especially appropriate for academic institutions. "In an organization with many highly educated professionals with considerble expertise of their own, the president needs to . . . help each professional be his or her own planner and innovator" (Keller, 1983, p. 124). Empowerment is antithetical to classical organizational management; it is the core of intrapreneurial leadership. Empowerment is a vision of people contributing willingly to the successful future of an organization.

Peters and Waterman (1982) have a sophisticated appreciation of people and their need to count, belong, be competent, be cared for, be visible—all basic human needs. People must matter all of the time, not just in times of organizational crisis. Time after time in describing *Break-Throughs* Nayak and Ketteringham (1986) emphasize the importance of people. In the story about polypropylene, one of the protagonists says that " . . . a manager's most important supervisory function is in choosing the best people to do the job" (p. 312). In the same book the production manager for the Sony Walkman, Kozo Oshone, says: "The personnel choices one makes at the beginning of a project are basic. Nothing is more important" (p. 324). It is people who count.

The pivotal strategic resource for organizations is now people, not dollar capital. Leadership, for example, implies people, a human business, a personal business. People are so important that Pinchot (1985) states he would rather have a class A person with a class B idea than vice versa. What he is saying is that it is the person (the intrapreneur) who takes an idea and makes it a reality. It is the person who is responsible for success. Empowerment is the tool which facilitates such accomplishments.

Empowerment as a process does not imply absolute freedom for people to do as they choose. Real empowerment takes place within the singular vision or mission of an organization.

To be effectively empowered, people need power: information, support, and resources (Kanter, 1983a). Power is the reciprocal of leadership; it is what translates intention (vision, meaning, and strategy) into reality and sustains that reality. Power is the ability to get obstacles out of the way so that others can use their own power (be empowered) to get the job done. Kanter (1983a) believes that innovation is 90 percent acquisition—the acquisition of power to move beyond a formal job charter and influence others.

This notion of getting out of the way so others can be visible, do what is relevant, contribute, and work hard is an important one. Managers control; leaders articulate and communicate a vision and empower others to "make it happen." To be sure, leaders in an organization do not abdicate their responsibilities; they are still responsible for decisions and outcomes. But leaders depend on others in their organization to meet these goals, to make the vision become a reality.

In academic organizations, the goal is to empower and enable faculty (and others) to assist in strengthening the institution in ways which " . . . satisfy the needs of both the professor and the college" (McMillen, 1987, p. 15). We disagree that advances in academia are made over the dead bodies of resisting professors. Dramatic whole-institution steps forward are relatively rare in large academic institutions (Jellema, 1986), yet such progress is what occurred at our University because of the faculty, not in spite of it.

Intrapreneurs take the lead in supporting and shaping empowerment. " . . . they have the courage of their trust in the others around them" (Deal and Kennedy, 1982, p. 154). Thus, empowerment is far more than delegating. One can delegate all day and night and never empower anyone. Empowerment implies that, deep down, at the bottom line, when all the frills are stripped away, those who empower really trust people to get something done. Thus empowerment takes place in fiscally good times and bad. People are not given autonomy and discretion only when it is fiscally affordable and then reined in when the times get tight. Either people are empowered or they are not. The issue of empowerment is really a culture issue, a basic issue of how one views the world.

It is clear that empowerment and intrapreneurial efforts are intimately related. Intrapreneurship is impossible in an organization if people cannot be empowered to be intrapreneurs. The shopping list of empowerment commodities (information, resources, support) summarizes what intrapreneurs need to be successful. This list is complete despite its short, three-item length, although the items are not easy to acquire. More than anything else, intrapreneurs need empowerment to act if they are to succeed.

LEARNING

Empowerment implies mastery and competence. Learning how to learn may be the most important skill in the new information society. As such, organizations may take on education functions because their members need opportunities and resources to learn. If the greatest opportunity for improvement is people, then people development may be a growth industry.

A learning environment in an organization implies stretching, breaking new ground, and creativity. Learning to do things in new ways is valued and takes place without the press and stress of crisis. Most organizations can learn to do things differently and in new ways if the only alternative is to die.

In another sense, in an empowered organization the value of learning implies that there is a tolerance for mistakes. After all, this is how one learns. But this tolerance is a paradox. The tight side of the organization wants to minimize mistakes and maximize efficiency. However, the loose side of the organization, that side dealing with ambiguity, intrapreneurship, leadership, and change must tolerate mistakes, for mistakes are unavoidable.

An intolerance for mistakes in an atmosphere of (supposed) empowerment leads to the "Alice in Wonderland Organization." In this type of organization many employees may appear to be very creative, but in reality they will be extremely circumspect. The outcome of this cautiousness is that the probability of organizational success and survival falls. When supervisors and upper-level management symbolize the Queen of Hearts because of their "off with your head" messages, positive outcomes will be few and far between. People will fear the consequences of failing.

Even in organizations seriously motivated to genuinely empower their employees, empowerment can be difficult to implement. Empowering others can fail and the organization may not be able to break free from the power of inertia. We are probably all familiar with an entropic institution in which there is much frenetic activity, but few good products or successes. Institutions must be able to translate ideas and hard work into successful ventures.

RISK

Organizations which empower their employees must expect that these people will take risks. People empowered have, in essence, been given permission to serve the organization by not only better performing the activities listed under their job descriptions but in finding new and better solutions to organizational problems.

To take a risk creates or enhances the chance of some unfortunate occurrence—and of some positive occurrence. We risk the unpleasant to gain the desired. The issue in organizational functioning is not one of whether to take risks but whether to accept one risk versus another. In academic institutions, maintaining the status quo and doing "nothing" could be a very large risk in the years to come. In an empowered college or university, taking chances is an accepted part of institutional functioning.

The concept of risk is not a new notion in academia. Wriston (1959), in looking back over a long career as a College and University President stated:

American enterprise is supposed to be founded upon risk-taking; the risks should not be rash, but if some are not taken the system is nonsense. Academic advance does not come, for most institutions, without taking chances. Refusal to accept hazards is neither good business sense nor good educational statesmanship. (p. 112)

No great or successful university ever got that way by taking the safe path (Keller, 1983). Where is this academic tradition of risk taking today? Why have so many colleges and universities become so cautious and failure-averse? An empowering academic institution which tolerates risk would help the organization be more vital and successful.

For all we believe in academic intrapreneurship, it is not a guarantor of success; all ventures have risk and many will fail. For example, the return on an innovative venture can be zero percent or it can even be negative! The product (curriculum, course, etc.) may not contribute positively to the future quality or portfolio mix of the university. Intrapreneurship is a cross-turf beast. Attempting to get projects completed successfully may result in meddling which is counterproductive to the organization. Intrapreneurship can, even if it involves small increases in resources (people, funds, etc), cause these resources to be diverted to what turns out to be nonproductive activities.

But who leads and who follows? A university administration must be willing to risk; faculty must be willing as well. Who plays it safer? It is an interesting question. Can progressive intrapreneurial administrators lead a traditional faculty? Can a risk-taking faculty push administrators to act or to undertake new projects? Is one related to the other?

The risk of maintaining the status quo is great. Keller (1983), in his impassioned plea for strategic planning in academia, states convincingly that higher education as we know it will die without change. Thus, ours is a mixed message. Adequate rewards may not be present, but those working in academia cannot afford to wait for an external upside to risk. We have to be willing to do the right thing (even if difficult) for our academic organizations without any guarantees of more than a pat on the back. Empowerment demands that we behave so.

The intrapreneur needs to lead and to empower. But an intrapreneur also needs to understand how people make sense of what happens within an organization. It is the concept of culture, a third part of the intrapreneur's world, that we discuss in Chapter 5.

Chapter 5
Culture

What is most intriguing about organizational culture is the influence it has on the lives of those who live and work within its confines. This power extends to their perceptions, their desires, their goals, and their actions. (Riley, 1983, p. 435)

To ignore culture and move onto something else is to assume, once again, that formal documents, strategies, structures, and reward systems are enough to guide human behavior in an organization—that people believe and commit to what they read or are told to do. (Kilmann, Saxton, and Serpa, 1985, p. 422)

If intrapreneurs are to be successful, they must be sensitive to how individuals in organizations make sense of their experiences. " . . . the idea of culture focuses attention on the expressive, nonrational qualities of the experience of organization. It legitimates attention to the subjective, interpretive aspects of organizational life" (Smircich, 1983, p. 355). Culture supplements concepts of structure or technology with equally valid, but less frequently discussed, organizational realities such as shared understanding and beliefs, affect, values, norms, behaviors and practice, and assumptions of the world.

Culture is a continuous recreation of shared meanings. Members in any group, whether it is a business organization or religious commune, create and recreate their culture through their interactions, their shared interpretations, and the significance they attach to what occurs and what they experience. Culture can be manifest in the simplest behavior.

Culture in an organization floats in the air and affects everyone. It is the unseen determinant of organizational life. Culture is often mistaken for the organization's vision, mission, reward systems, history, transactions, and people. More accurately, it lies deep beneath these elements and shapes how we feel and how we perceive our organization. The values, myths, heroes, and symbols which mean something to people who work in an organization are a road map to culture. But often this map is difficult to read, more like a mosaic or tapestry than a topography which is drawn in a linear fashion with a key (and thus easy to read).

All groups have commonality. Groups must have a common language and shared conceptual categories. They must also have some way of defining boundaries, selecting members, and allocating authority, power, status, property, and other resources. Groups also need norms for interpersonal relationships and intimacy, criteria for dispensing rewards and punishments, and ways of coping with the unimaginable, unpredictable, and stressful event (Schein, 1985b). Culture, therefore, is omnipresent in any group of people; it defines the nature of things.

Culture determines how formal statements will be interpreted and provides that which written documents leave out. It impacts on an organization's performance and behavior, directing people toward or away from organizational goals. It varies in both its pervasiveness (how deep and widespread it is) and its strength (how compelling it is).

Because culture cannot be measured or captured easily, it was omitted from organizational theorizing and discussions until the last twenty years. The reasoning seemed to be that, if something could be measured, it was somehow rational and valid;

only recently has the importance of an organization's soul been emphasized or written about. It is this very soul which is intimately entwined with intrapreneurs.

CULTURE AS METAPHORS

Culture embodies deep and powerful themes communicated and understood as fairy tales, myths, taboos, sagas, and legends. For example, a corporation might perceive itself as a military army, destroying the enemy (competitor) and everything in its path. Or an institution might think of itself as a protagonist from a fairy tale in which good triumphs over evil and everyone (customers, students, etc.) lives happily ever after. The metaphor which permeates the organizational culture will affect intrapreneurs' strategies, decisions, and allocation of resources.

It is these metaphors and symbols that help people make unique sense of their settings and unite that which would otherwise be fragmented. In a sense, strategy helps organizations adapt to their metaphorical realities (Sapienza, 1985). Cultural metaphors can include, but are not limited to, organisms, machines, the social realm (theaters, dramas), political arenas, order (metaphors on orderliness), fairy tales, games, religion, science, the military, and journeys. The application of metaphors to organizations is but the latest use of symbols in understanding various dimensions of human existence. Intrapreneurs provide leadership, in part, through the power of their metaphors.

RITES AND RITUALS

A strong culture has ceremonies—visible and potent examples of what the organization stands for. It has storytellers and priests who interpret, tell, and maintain the organization's saga. It has rites and rituals (day-to-day activities) which are meaningful at a symbolic level.

Rituals are physical expressions of cultural values and beliefs. For example, Deal (1985) argues convincingly that people need ways of understanding and mourning the passing of the old—"ritual dances of culture." Whether this is a spontaneous testimonial affair for a valued member who is leaving the organization (representing a passing culture), to the bronzing of a typewriter which is being replaced by new word processors, people need ways to remember fondly that which is dying or dead. Since the goal and content of rites and rituals help reinforce culture, intrapreneurs will find many uses for them.

Colleges and universities have a well-established, powerful set of rites and rituals. Whether it is commencement, convocation, new student week, colloquium, or a host of other ceremonies, we remind ourselves often of what we are all about. But a university can have a "gorgeous" set of rituals (pomp and circumstance) and still offer a rotten educational product. A university can have a strong culture (e.g., we all get along without discord) which does not help it address external or internal realities. Much of academic culture may be counterproductive to a vital institutional future. Academic intrapreneurs may have to introduce productive rites and rituals into their organizations.

HEROES

Heroes are people who have found their way into the organizational culture. By their acts, heroes create and maintain an intrapreneurial culture. They are tolerant of risk taking, for example. Perhaps institutions of higher education lack intrapreneurship and cultures which would be productive because, in part, they lack contemporary heroes. Educational organizations have few current heroes; even fewer are recognized as such. We are the worse for this. Higher education needs heroes to lead its institutions if it is to have strong cultures and sagas to tell. If work is to be meaningful for faculty, they need heroes. It is heroes who provide a lasting influence in an institution.

VALUES

Values are the bedrock of any corporate culture, the essence of a company's philosophy for success. They capture the imagination, provide direction for day-to-day behavior, and guide the making of choices. In an organization with a strong culture,

the philosophies are alive; they become the collective unconscious (archetypes) for the corporation. Organizations must have
well-thought-out, passionately felt values that give people
meaning. Only then is a strong, positive, intrapreneurial culture possible.

EXAMPLES OF CULTURAL COMPONENTS WHICH FACILITATE INTRAPRENEURSHIP

Culture which supports intrapreneurial efforts includes (1)
earned respect—a sense that the enterprise is special in what it
stands for, what it does and how it does it, and demands and
deserves uncommon effort and contribution from those who
work on the project; (2) the knowledge that people will be dealt
in, not excluded; (3) an appreciation for and high respect for
evangelical zeal; and (4) the feeling that profit is an outcome of
what one does, not the end in and of itself.

Organizations interested in using intrapreneurship might want
to pay special attention to some examples of culture provided
by Clifford and Cavanagh (1985). A notion such as "if it ain't
been fixed, it will break" implies relentless attention to detail,
people, structure, and process. A second idea is that "if things
work well they can work better." A third is "always solidly
anchor a vision in reality." This allows the vision to be clear
and easily seen.

Loose–Tight

One important, valid, and useful culture in an organization
which values intrapreneurship is Loose–Tight. In an organization with such a culture the control systems are congenial
(Waterman, 1987) and facilitate productivity and new ventures.
An organization needs simultaneously the discipline necessary
to execute day-to-day activities and the freedom to adapt to a
changing world. It needs superior scanning, data collection,
analysis and information, and unending focus on efficiency. Yet
at the same time it must be able to deal with larger issues of
effectiveness, culture, mission, leadership, empowerment, and

vision. The loose side and a superbly managed and productive tight side can both be firmly anchored in culture.

Many colleges and universities seem to forsake the looseness and keep only the tightness, adopting what Deal and Kennedy (1982) call a "process culture" with a focus on bureaucracy. In an organization with a process culture, process and caution become very important. In successful organizations with a bias to action, one will usually find a culture of looseness and tightness.

In summary, the loose–tight phenomenon is best described as "vision and empowerment with structure." Clifford and Cavanagh (1985) call it synchronization. What is loose is loose and what is tight is tight and both work interdependently to serve common institutional goals.

THE PAST

"Change-oriented administrators are particularly prone to act as though the organization came into being the day they arrived. This is an illusion, an omnipotent fantasy. There are no clean slates in established organizations. . . . There can be no change without history, without continuity" (Bennis, 1975, p. 333).

Culture is part of a group's collective unconscious; it contains organizations' archetypes. The past contains the heroes and myths which make up the culture's fabric. A strong culture does not come about because of managerial action; it evolves through shared history. The past is important because intrapreneurs must understand the organization's culture if they are to succeed; if violations of organizational traditions and culture must take place, intrapreneurs must understand the radical nature of what they are proposing to do. Understanding past events, people, decisions, structure, reward systems, relationships, and strategy (especially in response to crisis or other critical events) is a good way of understanding prevailing organizational culture. The history of a college or university yields information about its culture's genesis, stability, and consistency.

Changing culture takes patience and time; cultures are evolutionary, not revolutionary. There is no quick fix to many organizational problems, culture included. Converting abstract ideas into successful concrete realities requires a long-term view of time and accomplishment. One must have a sense of history and the past. The intrapreneur, especially in educational institutions, will confront a strong set of deeply hidden cultural values.

The past may have cobwebs; the challenge is to sweep the attic of the past clean, to open the windows in this attic so light shines in, and then to move foward. The past is intimately linked to both the present and future, but not always positively. It is helpful to understand the past because an organization's culture which is currently unproductive may have once been profitable and vital.

Organizations can be slaves (victims) to their past or they can be masters of change (Kanter, 1983a). An understanding of the past enables intrapreneurs to move freely and confidently through the invisible cultural corridors of an organization. After all, culture shapes our commitment, our effort, and our happiness. It demands the intrapreneur's attention.

But there are other organizational dimensions which also command the intrapreneur's attention. We are almost through our brief description of the intrapreneur's world. All that remains is to discuss the organization itself.

Chapter 6
Organizational System Variables

Intrapreneurship takes place within an organization or institution and it influences and is influenced by a host of organizational dimensions. We focus on five such organizational system variables most relevant for the intrapreneur. These are rewards, technology, value, bureaucracy, organizational structure, and strategic types.

REWARDS

The college or university which values empowerment must reward its productive and contributing intrapreneurs with many things *besides* salary, especially because adequate and sufficient financial remuneration (merit pay, performance bonuses, profit sharing) is often impossible in and of itself. Appropriate rewards include recognition (recognition rituals), resources (people, funds, space), and autonomy and power (the opportunity to innovate again). The empowered faculty member seeing a pet idea taken to its logical end point may experience this as an intrinsic reward. Allowing faculty and administrators (most of whom were and still are faculty) to test the reality of a dream by reducing a teaching load, changing a teaching schedule or teaching responsibilities, or gaining student employees for a project may all be rewarding.

The idea that academic intrapreneurs should be allowed to earn their own venture capital (Pinchot, 1985) has merit. If not permitted to do so, it will lead to a condition that Keller (1983) describes as academic hokum, the incessant talk about new ideas and information with no monies put aside for new ventures. "Bluntly, an institution espousing alertness, flexibility for new opportunities, and strategic initiatives, needs to put some of its money where its mouth is" (p. 168). The empowerment of intrapreneurs with their own resources allows people, using their experience, to choose the avenue which best meets the needs of their organization.

The issue of adequate rewards for intrapreneurs and members of their intrapreneurial team is a vexing problem for institutions of higher education. Solving this problem takes creativity. A good way to start may be to ask potential intrapreneurs for a wish list or smorgasbord of rewards which they perceive to be of value.

TECHNOLOGY

Technology is the systematic management, functioning, or understanding of any part of an organization. The differentiation between what is *technical* and what is *technology* is important. A technical perspective includes the scientific and mechanical. Technology, on the other hand, is "the systematic treatment of an art" (Clifford and Cavanagh, 1985, p. 221); it is not necessarily technical.

Technology includes anything that is done in a systematic, repetitive, predictable way. Much of the functioning and management of colleges and universities involves technology. For example, one could include registration, financial aids, record-keeping, payroll, allocating resources, faculty teaching loads, faculty development, or reward systems in the technology domain. These are the "ruts" of the organization. They supposedly support behaviors on the part of the academic organization's members which move the institution closer to its goals.

Understanding technology's place in academia has been neglected. A perspective on technology allows new ways of understanding organizational functioning to unfold and bloom.

Technology, then, is not just computers; it is procedures, habits, paper forms, publishing contracts, and so on. Ideally, it is the part of the university that is unseen. However, a failure to understand technology can overwhelm the academic intrapreneur who has no real sense of what it takes to make an organization function in a generally orderly way, and according to a preagreed schedule.

The S-Curve

It is widely held that every technology must eventually be replaced by a superior one (adapted to the environment). A technology which is currently in place should be viewed as an "enabling" technology; it allows development and implementation to move forward. This is why, in part, we believe it may be desirable to fix something even it it is not broken. If an organization, its research and development staff, or its intrapreneurs do not develop a newer technology, a competitor will find a new enabling technology and cause the former organization to lose its niche in a product or service line.

Typically, in an academic setting the focus of technology is a human clientele (universities are service organizations) and so an intrapreneur must assess technologies in light of the client group (students, faculty, alumni, etc.) being addressed. Therefore, the technologies of higher education must be client-centered.

The S-curve is one visual way of understanding movement from a technology which has seen its day in the sun (was productive, allowed profit or good service to occur) to a new technology just starting out (will take resources and some effort before it realizes its potential). S-curves show the relationship between effort and performance for any technology under study or consideration. Figure 1 shows the relationship between one S-curve and another.

As a simple example of S-curves, consider the long history of the technology of communication. A full chronology of communication technology would require many S-curves lying next to each other. These would be S-curves representing such technological developments as nonverbal communication (sign lan-

Figure 1

S-Curves

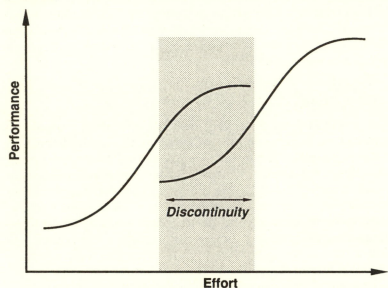

guage or smoke signals), use of written symbols, language development, telegraph and telephone, and computers, to name just a few. Usually only one pair of S-curves is shown together, representing the most recent technologies (old established and newly emerging [replacement]) for any given product, service, or process.

The space between two S-curves is called discontinuity. It takes new technology to make the passage between one curve and another. Transistors replacing vacuum tubes would be an example of crossing discontinuity to a new S-curve. Optics replacing wires in communications would be another. We have seen little, if any, discussion of S-curves and discontinuities in academic settings. Yet thinking in the language of technology and S-curves can be helpful in understanding both successes and failures in higher education. For example, television classes in college (1960s and early 1970s) were an unsuccessful move from one S-curve (a faculty lecturing live to a class) to another (lecture via television). Now we are told that with interactive communications this move across S-curves will be attempted again. Whether long-distance interative teaching is a successful technology will be interesting to watch.

The push in higher education seems to be for more and more efficiency, that is, doing more of the same, but better. Academic organizations must learn to recognize where they are on the S-curve for a variety of current technologies. Furthermore, they must examine these technologies with a critical eye. It is easy to see that tremendous amounts of effort, even if efficient, will not produce much more performance if a technology is a mature one and near the top of an S-curve.

What is needed for greater performance (project, better service, better problem solution) are new ways of doing business, that is, a leap from one S-curve to another. Recognizing the need to cross discontinuity is a necessary first step which, however, in and of itself will not ensure success. The choice of new technology must be correct, and the way the technology is applied and implemented (the work of intrapreneurs oftentimes) must be skillfully executed, or the new technology will not fit the consumer or will have little value. It will fail.

Limits

Every technology sets limits on what can be accomplished. Intrapreneurs are "limit breakers" in two meanings of the term. On the one hand, intrapreneurs can help an organization, using existing technologies, become more efficient and effective and move closer to its goals. Second, intrapreneurs also can move the organization closer to realizing its vision by helping it make the necessary journeys from one S-curve to another. Most academic organizations have not crossed the discontinuity chasm in many areas of organizational functioning such as registration, faculty development, curriculum, minority student recruitment, and retention. Unfortunately, what has worked well in the past is beginning to fail.

The problems which Boyer (1987) addresses in his book, *College: The Undergraduate Experience in America*, cry out for new solutions and technologies. The realization that limits are being reached, and insights into how new technologies can be utilized, will require that some academic organizations see what others see but to think what no one else has thought (Foster, 1986). New technologies will help some academic institutions provide an education with more value and quality than is presently offered, whether this is new and different approaches to freshman learning or how to teach students math and science. It also will give them a competitive advantage over their sister institutions.

All organizations must avoid what is called "Defender Hubris" (Foster, 1986). An organization is headed for disaster when false pride and stubbornness in sticking to the past or present prevent new, more adequate technologies and strategies from being implemented. But in higher education it seems almost impossible to get rid of the past, even if it has *not* worked!

Limits and technology beg the issue of smoke, image, and appearances. What is needed is real change, not the repackaging of old wine into new bottles.

VALUE

Products of any kind, established or new, are not successful solely because of high-quality workmanship or because they are a good buy for the money. Well-built horseless carriages would find few customers today. Ultimately, products or services are successful because customers perceive them as having value in their lives, as being meaningful and necessary. The predictions from the mid-1970s about future college enrollments were in error because a greater percentage of high school graduates began attending institutions of higher education, and more adults than ever were returning to them. The perceived value of a college education had gone up in our society.

This idea of value gives great meaning to the selection of intrapreneurial projects and to their success or failure in academic (or any) settings.

Sometimes products of value are expensive. The experience curve, that is, riveting the organization on efficiency (doing things cheaper) can be a road of good intentions doomed to fail. The low-cost producer produces more, more cheaply. What is not true, however, is that rational economic men and women necessarily buy the cheapest. An obsession with efficiency blinds an organization to innovation and intrapreneurship. A medium- or long-term view must be taken. In the end, value wins.

This concept of value is critical for colleges and universities which seem to be worshipping the god or goddess of efficiency. It is a false idol and institutions of higher education would better spend their time determining if what they do has any value for their students, region, and society. Cost may be a secondary issue. Since resources are limited in any organization, especially in public academic institutions, intrapreneurs can help these institutions produce services with high value with the limited resources available.

BUREAUCRACY

A bureaucracy is faceless, seemingly mindless, and passionless. It stares blankly in the face of an obvious need to act. As such, one would expect bureaucracy to be a pariah in colleges and universities, organizations in which people, their ideas, and their dreams are the chief currency. Yet, often bureaucracy thrives in academic institutions.

Bureaucracy, uncontrolled and uncaring, is the mortal enemy of intrapreneurs and their realization of good ideas. Bureaucracies are not easily dismantled, even when the need for which they were built has long gone, and they continue to sap precious resources.

Bureaucracy smothers innovation and substitutes rules for intrapreneurial common sense. It works against people taking responsibility and being empowered (Block, 1987); it stultifies decision-making and strait-jackets initiative (Clifford and Cavanagh, 1985).

Bureaucracy can put up numerous and powerful barriers to innovation (Betz, 1987; Kanter, 1983a; Quinn, 1985b). For example, organizational budgeting and accounting practices may so control people's behaviors that intrapreneurship is severely hindered.

Historically, bureaucracies and hierarchies existed within and helped create stable environments. It was the balance and equanimity which bureaucracies maintained that was valued.

Now, however, such stability is less valued; organizations must be unfrozen. Mueller (1987) sees a major challenge to management in its ability " . . . to open up the system to networking and unconventional thinking while still maintaining control" (p. 51).

Mueller's practice of having a file which includes people who "really know" and whose knowledge he respects is sage advice to the intrapreneur. It is intrapreneurs, acting as leaders, who must help others overcome bureaucracies so those who have been empowered can move ahead in the quest of their ideas.

ORGANIZATIONAL STRUCTURE AND STRATEGIC TYPES

Intrapreneurship, by definition, is a process which takes place within an organization. As intrapreneurs weave their way through the organizational labyrinth, it is helpful to have an understanding of different organizational structures and strategic types. It is well known that all that happens within an organization, including intrapreneurship, is influenced by the organization's structure.

Structure includes the rules, policies, procedures, customs, units, and relationships among departments and the design of the various functions within an organization. All of these structural specifications in an organization are intended to help it function efficiently and effectively, making a profit or serving a given clientele well.

Structure may be thought of as the total master plan of a formal organization which lays out how things should be.

Intrapreneurs require power, that is, resources, support, and information. They often work across unit boundaries and are involved with new ventures and products. Therefore, they must understand organizational structure; it is by working within or outside of their organization's structure that they will either surmount obstacles in their path or be defeated.

The model proposed by Miles and Snow (1978, 1984) is an excellent place to begin in order to gain an understanding of the organization in which one works. Their model includes strategic organizational types identified as Reactor, Defender, Prospector, and Analyzer.

The *Reactor* Organization is a passive responder to external forces acting on it, and may be in crisis because of this. Reactors may survive because by chance alone they align themselves successfully with their environment and market. It is a poor strategy, even for public institutions.

A classic example of a Reactor Organization was American Motors. Manfacturers of small cars, American Motors sold its products largely because it filled a niche for small, fuel-efficient automobiles which other automobile companies ignored. American Motors did not actively defend its niche and gave its customers, external environment, and product little active attention. For a while, the corporation was lucky. American Motors seemed to have no view of the future, no good feel for its customers, and few, if any, proactive strategies for long-term survival and success. When the fuel crisis arrived in America in the early 1970s and its competitors focused on its niche, American Motors was doomed. It held on for a decade, only to be taken over by Renault of France. It was then bought and disbanded by Chrysler Corporation. Its inabilities to make adjustments and create or defend its markets contributed to its going out of business. There are many academic institutions with "American Motors" written all over them.

The *Defender* is an organization with a narrow product-market domain. It does not look for opportunities and seldom needs to make major adjustments in technology, structure, or method of operation. Defenders are "steady on course," operating in a stable market or environment.

Defenders will defend their niche to the last breath. In this sense they can be very proactive, alive organizations. Think of McDonald's restaurants when you think of a successful Defender. Efficiency is their goal, bureaucracy their structure of choice.

However, to find a successful niche requires great expertise with effectiveness: "What do people want and value?" There is a place for intrapreneurs in a Defender Institution.

The Defender organization wants to repeat what it already knows. This used to be the sine qua non of a college or university and can be a successful strategy. Unfortunately, many public universities are neither efficient nor effective, so the argument that one should leave them alone to practice their current Defender organizational behaviors does not make sense. If they are Defenders, their goal should be to become good Defenders. However, many colleges and universities are too traditional and too bureaucratic in the bad sense of the terms to accomplish this without significant change. Many do not know what their niche is because effectiveness questions have not been posed. It is impossible for them to thrive.

Prospector organizations continually search for market opportunities. This is the experimenting, new-is-good, intrapreneurial organization at its extreme. This organization type thrives on ambiguity, change, and uncertainty. Texas Instruments was a successful Prospector before its unsuccessful foray into the personal computer business. There are few colleges or universities which would fit the Prospector model.

In an *Analyzer* organization, the old and existing must be separated organizationally from the new. This organization is a combination of a Defender and a Prospector. There are stable product lines and parts of the organization which are traditionally managed. But there also are more turbulent areas which readily adapt and adopt. The trick with an Analyzer is to successfully lead and manage an organization which has such a dual personality.

Most large doctoral institutions are Analyzers. We believe that the Analyzer should be the organizational model of choice for many universities, and that even regional universities such as our own might want to "loosen up enough" to allow some prospecting within their hallowed Defender halls.

If regional universities, which typically are members of state systems, cannot position for new programs in an Analyzer fashion, how can these state systems best serve their customers and society in general? And who is to lead state systems into a strong position for the future? Can state systems afford not to permit their regional universities to be Analyzers? However, to be an Analyzer, these institutions would need the capacity to identify S-curves and limits as well as the capacity to cross discontinuity. So much of what they do, their culture, and their technology would have to change.

In summary, to the extent that the world of tomorrow is similar to that of today, the defender is ideally suited for its environment. However, we believe common sense (and the rash of Blue Ribbon reports) tells us that this will not be the case. Clearly, the academic world of tomorrow will not be similar to that of today. It is more likely that the next 20 years will bring as many or more changes for higher education than the past 100 years. If this happens, those institutions which are Defenders will find their organizational structures part of their problems and difficulties. Keeping the same administrative structure and people tends to produce solutions which reflect variations on traditional themes, a situation which may not work for very long.

Academic institutions must be prepared to move from being Reactors to Defenders and from being weak Defenders to strong Defenders or Analyzers. These changes and transitions will require more than mere changes in organizational structure. They will require commitment and attention to all that we discussed earlier in the book—leadership, effective and appropriate culture, empowerment, and especially vision and meaning.

CONCLUSION

There are limitations to intrapreneurship and organizations' abilities to thrive and be productive. The intrapreneurial process is a complex one with numerous opportunities for failure. Intrapreneurs or innovators usually have to be right the first time; they seldom get a second chance for any one idea or project. Windows of opportunity close and opportunities are lost forever. Bad things do happen to good companies. The marketplace, economics, discontinuities which are poorly understood or managed, strategic errors, competition, and organizational weaknesses all can impair success. Organizations and the work they do are complex. Products vary in number, technology, rate of innovation, and integration; the market can be geographically small or large, with complicated distribution channels and many types of customers. Intrapreneurs need some luck if they are to succeed.

It is not just complexity which can defeat an organization's attempts to meet the future successfully. Top-level managers may choose the wrong vision, provide insufficient leadership, be unable to empower others, avoid risks, not be trusted, or not understand the power of culture.

To experience the intensity of success, institutions of higher education must be willing to examine themselves critically; they must come to know what type of organizations they are, and they must understand their individual strengths and weaknesses. Academic institutions must make a decision if they wish to be Entrepreneurial Corporations (Clifford and Cavanagh, 1985). The vision of what they can be drives intrapreneurship. We believe that they can no longer be complacent or content.

Now that we have completed an Overview of Intrapreneurship in Academe and a summary of The Intrapreneur's World it is time to turn to a case example of academic intrapreneurship in action. Part III presents this description of "The Doing."

PART III

THE DOING

Chapter 7
In the Beginning

An organization's past is an important element in the intrapreneurship process. Thus, understanding something about the history of our University is essential in order to fully appreciate the period of crisis which spawned the intrapreneurial efforts detailed in several of the remaining chapters.

THE NORMAL SCHOOL ERA (1871–1959)

Our University, founded in 1871, has its roots in the Era Of The Normal School (1839–1900). Like other normal schools, it had as its sole mission the training of teachers. Despite two name changes—from Normal School to State Teachers College (1927) and then to State College (1951)—its course was never altered.

Virtually all normal schools, and their retitled successors, were administered by "principals" (who came and went frequently) and small teaching staffs. Unlike the situation at colleges and universities with a more traditional academic history, little authority was granted to the faculty of normal schools.

Oshkosh, with one notable exception, was no different. The notable exception was that Oshkosh had great stability in its leadership as only five presidents and two acting presidents served prior to 1959. The presidential leadership tended to be "paternalistic," "authoritarian," even "patriarchal" (Peterson, 1978). Decision-making during this period was modeled after the public secondary schools, with the president functioning as the sole decision-maker on virtually all matters the regents did not oversee.

In addition, Wisconsin had a long tradition of having its Board of Regents (which oversaw all normal schools) comprised of a representative from each school's immediate geographic area. Oshkosh's representatives strongly resisted any change in the school's mission as a teacher training college. The regents' involvement in the school's affairs represented the kind of paternalism which was fairly typical of the Normal School System. For example, they not only selected the school's president, but they often screened applications and interviewed other prospective employees. Furthermore, they frequently put their stamp of approval on all promotion and salary lists.

This eighty-eight-year period of the school's history was a time of a limited, but clear, teacher training mission, a reasonably supportive community environment, and a stable, if not lean, resource base. It was an era in which its presidents exercised strong, traditional leadership. Enrollment was stable, growing as the region's population grew, from 173 in 1871 to just over 2,000 in 1959. Expectations on the part of the legislature, the regents, the administration, and the students were compatible. There was limited faculty mobility. By 1931 there were fifty-six faculty, thirty-one of whom had been employed at Oshkosh for more than twenty-five years. In 1959 the number of faculty totaled 102. Even as this period drew to a close the school's values tended to be sacred and parochial. "There was an almost 19th century emphasis on values, tradition, and the certitude of the school's mission" (Peterson, 1978, p. 195).

THE STATE UNIVERSITY PERIOD (1959–1974)

During the next fifteen years the school experienced unprecedented growth of its resource base, both in terms of students and state funding. The school's mission, which had been so clear since its inception, became fragmented and disjointed.

The name changes which the school underwent during this

era are reflective of the school's struggle with its identity and mission. In 1964, after several graduate programs were added, Wisconsin State College became Wisconsin State University. "The change of name to 'state college' came often as a recognition of a fait accompli, rather than as an expression of intention for the future" (Wahlquist and Thornton, 1964, p. 13). Such was the case of Oshkosh.

Then, in 1971, with the merger of the Wisconsin State University System and the University of Wisconsin System, the school became the University of Wisconsin Oshkosh. Legislatively, this made the school a copartner with the state's flagship (doctoral) campus. Merger raised expectations and aspirations. In reality it gave us a Chancellor instead of a President.

Evolution from normal school to state college to university was an inevitable part of a national trend. The University's situation during most of this period can be conceptualized, in part, as a conflict over the organizational identity or mandate of the institution. Without a reasonably high level of consensus as to the organization's goals, and without leadership to help set goals and resolve conflicts, there was no clear mission and the organization was, to a large degree, turned over to external environmental forces to shape its identity. The University's fundamental teacher-training mission was being challenged, as the organization was now expected to adapt to meet the growing social and economic aspirations of working-class America, which was enrolling its children in record numbers.

The rush of new students brought new enrollment peaks to Oshkosh, including many more students who decided not to teach but to become businessmen, scientists, or engineers, or to be prepared to continue graduate study. Enrollment skyrocketed from just over 2,000 in 1959 to almost 12,000 by 1971. The next steps were inevitable: to expand the campus, to augment the library and laboratories, to add to the numbers and backgrounds of the faculty (the number of faculty increased from 102 in 1959 to 677 by 1971), and to seek authorization for a broad range of liberal arts majors.

The University's unprecedented growth cannot be attributed to astute leadership but was largely a result of demographic and social factors. As Keller (1983) states, "demography is to a considerable extent destiny" (p. 12). For example, the city of Oshkosh had a drinking age of eighteen years. Moreover, drinking establishments were built proximate to campus. The campus became a great attraction for young people who were looking to have a good time. As might be expected, this soon gave the University the reputation of being a "party school." While this may have fueled enrollments in the short run, this image would eventually become a millstone around the University's neck that would take many years to undo.

In addition, the external conflicts of the 1960s—the Vietnam War, the draft, racial disturbances—affected the internal functioning of the University and the almost symbiotic relationship it had with the community and region. The administration was unprepared and unequipped to handle these factors.

Decision-making paralysis and lack of leadership became acute problems. Important decisions were delayed as long as possible. The three senior administrators would meet with the President and each would argue for a particular decision. No decision would be made, and each would then approach the President individually—whoever saw him last often was able to prevail (Peterson, 1978).

While it was a time ripe for change there was little chance that any major changes (besides growth) would occur. Administrative replacements were chosen from among those who viewed the organization in a traditional way and who had been observed long enough to make reasonably certain that their behavior was acceptable to existing norms. (This is a strategy designed to maintain the present culture.) The top-level administrators who were in charge throughout this period had been hand-picked by the existing administration, with no faculty involvement. High value was placed on longevity, institutional loyalty, and a low profile. One might characterize the dominant coalition as epitomizing the good old boys' club.

A very strong external force which was prominent throughout this period was System Administration. It was System Administration, not the faculty, which had selected the University's President in 1959. Furthermore, the University administration was heavily dependent on System Administration to provide direction, and it tended to view *that* group as its major constituent rather than the growing numbers of students, faculty, or regional citizens and communities. There was, perhaps, even an element of overrespect for System Administration authority. After the Kent State incident there was a request from some faculty and students to lower the flag in honor of the dead students. One administrator called System to ask for direction.

During this period it was as if the administration believed it was the beneficiary of the "Tooth Fairy Syndrome" as described by Charles Levine—the belief that, if they continued to muddle along as they had in the past, some benefactor (System Administration) would somehow miraculously appear to keep things going or to restore happy days (Keller, 1983). The history of strong Regent and System Administration involvement in the operation of the University prevented the development of in-house organizational and administrative processes and strategies that would provide a sound management base for decision-making and problem solving.

As the faculty and student body grew in size and changed qualitatively during the late 1960s, the gap between leadership and its constituent groups grew wider and wider. The leadership, which had been chosen by an external agency (System Administration) no longer reflected the values of the people they were to administer and serve.

The strong driving forces within the school for greater status, as reflected in the demand for hiring faculty with stronger academic credentials, created much tension and conflict with the largely passive administration. A former administrator is quoted as saying:

I believe that things started going so fast in terms of growth that the guys in charge were just hanging on to stay with it. When you hang on like that you're more concerned with hanging on than looking where you're going and as a result there got to be a lot of other passengers . . . and then all of a sudden these other passengers tried to steer the train or at least they wanted their presence recognized. (Peterson, 1978, p. 74)

While typically the older, more prestigious members of a faculty tend to have a strong influence on a campus and help to shape its direction, this assumes that younger faculty are likely to want to emulate their elders. This was not true in our case. The newer faculty were likely to have had more formal education than the "old guard," and the newer faculty had been socialized by their research-oriented professors during their graduate training. They had little professional respect for a faculty who had been granted tenure as a consequence of longevity rather than the result of the then-traditional academic reward system.

Not only was there conflict within the ranks of the faculty, but there was a growing and widespread hostility toward the conservative, paternalistic, and ineffective administration. This created a volatile atmosphere on campus. The new, more formally trained younger members of the faculty had their cosmopolitan values jolted by administrative actions (all of which took place in the 1960s and all of which are understandable if one thinks of a small, quiet teacher's college of another era) such as:

- requiring that all supplies be ordered through the President's Office;
- having a business manager refuse to pay for a nude model for art classes unless ordered to by the President;
- receiving a memo from the Dean of the College that laid out a dress code for faculty which read in part: "Large Universities may tolerate a few eccentrics who delight in a bizarre appearance of unusual haircuts and beard growths, open shirts, and colored vests but in colleges the size of ours there should be no encouragement of the beatnik whose marks are unkempt hair and beard and slovenly dress." (Peterson, 1978, p. 70)

The large enrollments of the 1960s brought increased numbers of minority students to a University and community that was virtually all-white. Unfortunately, there was a general lack of planning and attention given to the needs (academic, social, personal) of these students.

On November 21, 1968 (to become known on-campus as "Black Thursday"), a time not long after the urban riots in the summer of 1967 and the April 1968 assassination of Martin Luther King Jr., about ninety black students entered the President's office and presented a list of nonnegotiable demands. When the demands were refused, some of the protestors destroyed files, records, and desks. Police were called and arrests were made. Eventually the Administration suspended ninety of the protestors for the remainder of the school year. Many faculty who had been unhappy with the University administration for a variety of reasons became upset with the manner in which the Administration responded to the students and the general way in which the entire situation had been handled. In a heated faculty meeting after the student demonstration one senior administrator said, "We should remember that the school is like a family and the administration and central administration are the parents and the faculty are the children, and they should accept the decisions which were made in their behalf" (Peterson, 1978, p. 71). Faculty now had a major issue around which to focus their discontent.

The incident also caused a great wound in the school's relationship with a community and region that was very conservative in nature and very " . . . wary of the influx of new professors who were unlike themselves, and the minority students, no matter how relatively small their numbers" (Peterson, 1978, p. 95). It was a wound that would not heal for a long time.

Another major institutional problem was faculty morale. By 1968, about 50 percent of the faculty had been at the institution less than two years. Trained and socialized at research-oriented schools, these new young faculty had lofty visions for Oshkosh, including an expanded curriculum with graduate and Ph.D. programs. As it became clear that Oshkosh was not going to be, as one administrator put it, "the Harvard of the West," the school's self-image (at least for the new faculty) began to suffer. As one University staffer observed: "UW–O is a six cylinder Chevy. Some people tried to take a Chevrolet and put a Rolls Royce grill on it. It just didn't fit" (Peterson, 1978, p. 96).

The difficulty with not achieving "Harvard" status, *and lacking an alternative identity with which to be reasonably comfortable*, is that many people, faculty and students alike, felt the school was nothing. During the late 1960s and the 1970s the campus suffered from an inferiority complex. In 1971, when its name changed to U.W.–Oskosh its logo was "UW–O" but the "O" for Oshkosh was translated by many students and faculty into a "Zero," as in UW–Zero, which stood for nothing.

All of the external pressures and internal issues may have been manageable and solvable but the University's dominant coalition seemed unable or uninterested in changing the direction of the school. In addition, the very inexperienced Faculty Senate, newly created in 1964, was ineffective and there was no way for the faculty to involve itself in the decision-making process of the University because of its traditional hierarchical administration. For change to occur, a cataclysmic event was needed. And one occurred!

The postwar enrollment fizzle, which would not affect most institutions until the mid-70s, struck an unprepared and unsuspecting University at Oshkosh in 1972 and 1973. The enrollment dropped from around 11,800 in 1971 to just over 10,400 in 1973. What made a bad situation even worse was the fact that System Administration, which, in the 1960s, had projected an eventual enrollment target of approximately 20,000, had revised their projections and were now forecasting that there would be further reductions, to a possible low of 9,000 in the next few years!

As the University began to lose its enrollment, it also began to lose its resource base. Consequently, as the enrollment dropped and the projections looked bleak, some untenured faculty members were released. Eventually, in April 1973, twenty-two tenured faculty were placed on lay-off status.

The disagreements between the faculty and administration now became less ideological and more related to a basic fundamental conflict—job security. The lack of confidence in and distrust of the administration, which had been growing during the 1960s, was greatly exacerbated by the prospect of further staffing reductions of tenured faculty and staff because of the projections for a continued enrollment decline. The organization was in serious difficulty; it needed leadership.

But, given its history, why, how, or who could affect the changes that were so necessary to save an institution which was perilously close to becoming the equivalent of bankrupt? The University had the why; it was in crisis and was, therefore, becoming an albatross to System Administration. The who and how would be an outsider, for an important way to bring about change is to bring in someone from outside the institution to make needed changes. As Hefferlin (1969) notes,

the newcomer seems crucial for academic change. He may come from outside higher education altogether. He may be exploring problems regardless of departmental and disciplinary boundaries. He may represent different values, different goals, a different culture than his predecessors. The recruitment of such individuals as catalysts of change accounts for much of the process of reform. (p. 48)

But how do you get an outsider when there is no orderly process in place for removing ineffective leadership? There was no choice but to wait until the Chancellor decided to retire.

Chapter 8
Caution: Intrapreneurs at Work

PRELUDE

The style of this chapter is one of personal recounting by one of the authors who participated in the intrapreneurship. We emphasize especially the first year when so much was accomplished. The work was difficult, exhaustive, and exhausting, fatiguing both the body and mind. If this chapter were a film, it would be in black and white.

Intrapreneurship can be understood from many dimensions and within many frameworks. As authors we were faced with a dilemma. How do we help readers who have never engaged in intrapreneurship gain the fullest understanding of its nature? In most of this book knowledge of intrapreneurship is acquired by the reader through explanation, description, and analysis. But intrapreneurship has a subjective epistemology. The goal of the present chapter is to assist the reader in personally experiencing the phenomenological, interpretive world of intrapreneurship. A feeling for the experience, richness, and intensity of intrapreneurship is what is important to us here.

We write of the Druids in the university as instrumental for change. The Druids were and are the faculty who mirror what the Druids were in Celtic society, guardians and teachers of knowledge, wisdom, and magic; those who harness passion in the service of ideas and the intellect. Druids are faculty members who want to make a difference in their students' lives, who love the world of ideas, research, and "truth." Druids are the best of faculty, contributing to a university through their thinking, writing, being, and especially teaching. They worship a life of the mind. The reader will note that when the Druids' perceptions or observations are recounted they are set in CAPITAL LETTERS. We wanted to differentiate the telling of our tale from the thoughts and mind-set of the Druid Faculty.

PROEM

(Text in the Proem and Postscript to this chapter is based on a grant proposal to the National Association of College and University Business Officers, Washington, D.C. [Birnbaum, 1976]).

> *In 1972, The University of Wisconsin-Oshkosh began operating under budgetary and enrollment constraints that, if continued, threatened to destroy its ability to function as a university. During 1972–75, enrollment dropped 10% and the University had to make severe financial cutbacks because its operating budget was based directly on student enrollment. Tenured faculty were laid-off; highly qualified probationary faculty were released; needed equipment was not purchased; departmental supplies were severely curtailed. Action was required to make more effective and efficient use of remaining resources and to locate new money to finance innovative programs critically needed for the organization's recovery.*
>
> *The University traditionally conducted two seventeen-week semesters and an eight-week summer session. The normal contract for faculty members required that they teach twenty-four credits during the two semesters of the nine-month academic year (usually twelve credits each semester). They received extra compensation for teaching during the summer session.*
>
> *The University, like many others, engaged in peak-load*

staffing. It had to have enough instructors to accommodate the enrollment at its highest point during the academic year (the Fall semester). Enrollment during the Spring semester normally dropped by about 9 percent, at which time the same number of faculty taught significantly fewer students.

Extra compensation for summer school cost the University nearly $500,000 in 1974 and peak-load staffing required more faculty members than would have been needed for the total academic year if an optimal staffing pattern had been possible. Years of cutbacks and staff reductions had, however, drawn all contracting flexibility from the personnel portfolio.

In Summer 1974, the faculty and staff began consideration of a series of interrelated institutional changes. These changes, going under the rubric of "Calendar" consisted of three closely interrelated decisions:

1. *A new academic Calendar, dividing the traditional seventeen-week semester into two seven-week and a three-week term, would be instituted. The Calendar promised much greater scheduling flexibility to both students and faculty.*

2. *Summer Session teaching (during either one or both of two four-week terms) could be included as part of the faculty member's regular load, with the proviso that the total weeks of service and credits taught in a twelve-month period would not exceed previous academic-year load responsibilities.*

3. *A Faculty Development Program providing extra compensation for faculty research and curriculum development projects selected on a competitive basis was to be established. These projects were to be conducted during calendar periods outside of the faculty member's annual load. The program was to be funded at a level of approximately 2 percent of the University's total annual instructional budget.*

Implementation of this series of changes rested ultimately on the outcome of an all-University referendum scheduled for November 1974. Following the general presentation of the

> *proposal to the University community in August, thirteen papers on various aspects of the proposal (many written by faculty members) were distributed to each faculty and staff member during the ensuing three months. The Chancellor met with each department to discuss its concerns. The Faculty Senate and the Oshkosh Student Association debated it. No other decision at the University ever involved as many people in such a comprehensive manner.*

And if a move towards unity was in train, there was only one body in Celtic society capable of advancing it. This was the Druids, not only more powerful than the chiefs themselves, but also through their own organization, capable of traversing the tribal bounds and so of resolving internal jealousies. The most natural way of bringing their objective about would be through promoting the worship of a single pantheon of unarguably 'Druidic' gods who, though they might not supplant them, would at least take precedence over the tribal ones. This would represent the ideological unification which is always the precondition to political unity. (Rutherford, 1978, p. 137)

It is very early in 1973. The deep Wisconsin winter chills to the bone. We do not feel well professionally, and we know it. The University's institutional researchers promote the idea that we all take two relatively new organizational research instruments developed by the Educational Testing Service from Princeton. They are called the IFI and the IGI: the Institutional Functioning Inventory and Institutional Goals Inventory. Why not? Maybe this will give us some indication of what is wrong at the University at Oshkosh. So we all sit uneasily for these inventories in a "self-study day." The results confirm that something is wrong. We score so low that no one wants to publish and discuss the results. And so we remain without clear notions of what remedies to apply.

Some say it is because we have ineffective leaders. But are Universities really SUPPOSED to have leaders? And if so, aren't WE supposed to be the leaders? But anyone who stands forward to lead now has lost his or her professional senses. All of the decisions are really tough ones. There is only bad news to spread around, not the type of news that will call the entrepreneurs back to action.

Our present and past campus administration is blamed by some. Others blame the chaotic administration of a newly merged University of Wisconsin System. Some of the veteran faculty blame the new crop of faculty (the fresh Ph.D.s) often hired by administrative staff in the professional "meat markets" associated with professional society meetings in the large cities far away. Some of the "new bucks" blame the veterans who still chair the departments and control the powerful departmental committees. Yet others lay the blame on the recently established Faculty Senate. In truth, the blame is to be laid on everyone and no one. Everyone . . . and No One.

And then (January 1973) some news . . . our Chancellor is retiring (in December). Some say it is forced. Some say he feels that new blood is needed. Some say he is tired. Maybe everyone is right.

As winter turns to spring the condition of the University worsens. Decision-making moves steadily outward into a strained and disordered organization. Decisions seek and find those willing to make them. There are many talking, but most ducking. A few continue to take on the tough problems and decisions. The Dean of Letters and Science is one of these. There are calls for a "referendum to evaluate the Dean." While this does not occur, his strong sense of responsiblity at this time eventually will cost him his job. Several in staff roles begin to function as line officers, and they also soon find that they must move on. In this struggle, those who conscientiously volunteer for action do not last to serve long.

And where are the faculty entrepreneurs? Where are the multiple "mini-hearts" that, when combined, pump the professional lifeblood of the University through its corridors and provide the energy to move forward to the dream? They are not to be seen. Some have simply left. Some have stayed, but they have lost faith. But some that are left resemble Druid priests coping with a rapidly receding and broken forest. They are in remote clans, keeping the faith, and providing whatever support they can to each other.

The first (ever, for us) Chancellor's search and screen committee is formed. They are good people, and they represent well the various segments of the organization. Even a few of the Druid clans are visibly represented. There are some local candidates who aspire to be the new leader, and the usual political games are played. The committee works closely with the leaders of the UW System in Madison.

Through this all, the image of the University deteriorates, even as we search for a new leader. More and more, it is referred to as UW–Zero . . . by those inside and outside of the University community. Now, even the Druids frequently refer to it as such. UW–Zero! At first lightly, as a sick joke. Then more seriously, as a dangerous reality. A national publication (its survey to gather information poorly done, but widely distributed) says we are a high school with ashtrays. UW–Oshkosh gains notoriety for the annual St. Patrick's day bash (drinking and carousing). Even Johnny Carson knows where Oshkosh is on St. Pats! THAT IS OUR IDENTITY. IF IT WERE NOT SO SAD, IT WOULD BE FUNNY. EVEN SO, WE LAUGH . . . BECAUSE GENUINE DRUIDS DO NOT WEEP. OURS IS A LIFE OF IDEAS. THERE ARE NO SAD IDEAS. Even the University logo looks like a "UW" with a goose egg.

The summer of 1973 sees several major struggles in the faculty community. One revolves around budget cuts ($1 million and twenty-two TENURED faculty are placed on "lay-off" status), and consideration, and reconsideration. . . . The sanctum of the tenured position is ravaged. Declining student enrollments have come to haunt and hurt us.

Another struggle affronts in a totally different way. The "administrators" are pushing a new general education program that features interdisciplinary "modules," new teaching methods, computer-based instruction, and all of the new toys in the educational marketplace. "We have the money," they say ". . . now why don't you come and teach in this enlightened fashion? This program will raise our enrollments, allow you to teach more efficiently, and move the University ahead!" The Druids watch silently from deep in their forests. The program will soon die.

The changes in the campus administration parallel those in the forests in the fall of 1973. A temporary leader arrives from the System Administration in Madison to "take charge." He asks for the resignations of all key administrative personnel.

"A matter of protocol," they are told. Some refuse. They will not be with us long.

Finally, as Thanksgiving approaches, the announcement that a new Chancellor will soon arrive. The committee comes to us with a new leader from New Jersey. He will begin early in 1974. But still the forests are receding. In December of 1973, an additional fourteen staff members are released.

It is February 1974. The University has a new Chancellor. He does not bring with him the credentials or mannerisms of a Druid . . . but he seems to understand them. WE KNOW HIM AS BOB. His first visible administrative decision is to turn off the hallway bells which mark the beginning and end of classes in every building. MAYBE HE DOES KNOW WHAT DISTINGUISHES A UNIVERSITY FROM A HIGH SCHOOL? Three weeks after beginning as Chancellor he announces in the University Bulletin that the Library will be open longer on Friday nights. This is another signal to the Druids . . . longer hours with a tight budget? THIS FELLOW IS DIFFERENT . . . YOUNG . . . LONG AND LANKY . . . GUTSY . . . WEARS A BEARD . . . HAS A DOG RUNNING ON THE UNIVERSITY GROUNDS. HE HAS AN ATTRACTIVE, YOUNG, MULTI-RACIAL FAMILY. AND HE IS VERY QUICK. BUT HE IS NOT A DRUID, IS HE? DRUIDS DO NOT HAVE DOCTORATES IN HIGHER EDUCATION ADMINISTRATION!

The University learns quickly that this Chancellor is capable of abrupt and decisive behavior. He distinguishes quickly and clearly between what he does and does not like. He supports what he likes, and ignores the rest. He says yes or no. A decision-maker is again responsible for forest management. Some of those who have been "filling in" in that role do not read the situation correctly. There will soon be problems associated with conflicts in authority. The individuals in front of the parade must make room for another, and his team. Some do not stand aside . . . they are soon on the sidewalk.

The Chancellor is also capable of poking fun . . . the kind of fun that sends messages and makes some uncomfortable. He nominates his dog to be an "Outstanding Educator" . . . and the dog is accepted. The story makes the *Chronicle of Higher Education!* Funny? Not for the "near Druids" among the faculty who have also applied and made it in recent years . . . and included this distinction in their credentials as they applied for promotion and tenure! A BIT ARROGANT . . . BUT YOU MUST ADMIT IT *IS* FUNNY!

In his decision-making, the Chancellor also shows courage. Some of the local banks will not participate in the new Federal Student Loan Program. So he switches the University business to banks that do. He also announces that only five of the thirty first-year faculty will not be reappointed to serve in the upcoming Fall semester. . . . And our budget is lower. IT'S A FINE LINE BETWEEN COURAGE AND STUPIDITY . . . TELL ME AGAIN . . . WHERE DOES THIS FELLOW COME FROM?

It is early spring of 1974. The Chancellor gives a speech announcing a "shuffle" in the University's administration. Two are lost. He also says that the fiscal problems are not resolved.

And within a handful of months, the latent fiscal crisis facing the organization again erupts . . . like a cancer that had been held (by cautious and caring hands in UW System Administration) in temporary remission. HOW WILL HE DEAL WITH IT? WILL WE HAVE MORE TENURE LAYOFFS?

There are LOTS of meetings and consultations. There are new procedures for the reassignment or layoff of tenured faculty . . . and more memos on fiscal policy related to layoffs. The Chancellor recommends to the Board of Regents that a "state of fiscal emergency" *not* be declared at UW Oshkosh. The Druids watch from deep in the forest. IS THIS A SIGNAL THAT THE DESTRUCTION OF THE FORESTS WILL CEASE? IS AN EFFORT IN THE WIND TO (SOMEHOW) STOP THE SYSTEMATIC INWARD MIGRATION OF THE FOREST EDGE?

Finally, in late spring of 1974, the news comes, and it is good. Severe austerity perhaps, but there will be no layoffs for 1975–76. The Chancellor makes his communication with the President of the System public for all to read.

Even with severe dollar problems the budget of the University is large. There is money to be allocated. And in the internal struggles for very scarce discretionary resources, some goes to the Druids, in very visible ways. The Deans have advocated some initiatives on the Druid's behalf, and won support for them. The support of UW System people in forestalling a fiscal exigency (an exigency would allow further layoff of tenured faculty) at the University makes it clear that there is a good working relationship between the Chancellor and some of his personal sponsors in "Central" (UW System Administration). But the new System Administration is still disorganized, and there are also good working relationships between some local administrators who aspired to be Chancellor and *their* contacts at System. More games are played. MORE BAD DECISION-MAKING BY SOME INDIVIDUALS . . . THERE WILL BE ONLY ONE LEADER OF THIS PARADE.

Now, in the late spring of '74, with the fiscal crisis in the background, the Chancellor makes his offensive strategy visible. The key idea revolves around individual choice and concepts of time. Do we view time as a slave or a master? He argues that each faculty member must be a master of his or her "professional time." He sees the traditional university calendar as an artificial constraint that enslaves our professional lives to a particular time structure. True, the entrepreneurial University of Wisconsin Madison faculty can escape the professionally strangling grip of a "teach nine months, regroup during three months" academic cycle. Those who can win the grants are freed . . . they can manage when they teach, and when, where, and how long they do professional research and study. The others do not get tenure. That's simple.

The Chancellor argues that, realistically, the situation for faculty at Oshkosh is different. He starts with the premise that we are DOOMED to teach twelve standard credit hours (maybe even more) per week. But he says that we can still beat the burden of that load by becoming *In*trapreneurial. Let's turn the time structure of the organization around and set it up so that it lets us free up and plan for "large blocks of time that we can devote to our professional lives."

ON THE FACE OF IT . . . A STRANGE IDEA. BUT THERE IS NO ONE ELSE TO LISTEN TO. HE IS NOT A DRUID . . . BUT HE SEEMS TO KNOW HOW IMPORTANT DRUIDS ARE TO A UNIVERSITY.

By coincidence, some on the campus have been moving on complementary ideas viewed from a student-learning perspective. "Self-Pacing" is a vogue to be explored. The Dean of L&S

has sponsored the idea for several years, and some of the Druids have emerged from the forest and are pursuing the notion in a highly visible program center. SEE, IT SEEMS TO WORK FOR SOME OF US . . . PERHAPS THE SHACKLES OF THE TRADITIONAL ACADEMIC CALENDAR CAN BE BROKEN . . . WE MUST THINK ABOUT THIS.

THIS NOTION OF "FLEX-PROFESSIONAL-TIME" IS AN UNCOMFORTABLE ONE . . . NONETHELESS IT MAY BE GOOD FOR SOME . . . BUT NOT FOR MOST DRUIDS. STILL, WE SHOULD SUPPORT THOSE OF US WHO ARE INVOLVED IN THIS PROJECT . . . PERHAPS WE CAN FIND A WAY IN THEIR SUCCESS FOR US TO REVITALIZE OUR PROFESSIONAL LIVES AND REALIZE OUR PROFESSIONAL DREAMS. Another good reason to listen.

And more discussion and thought on the Chancellor's idea. THERE IS NOT ENOUGH PROFESSIONAL TIME, THAT IS CERTAIN. SO WE MUST MANAGE WHAT WE HAVE MORE INTENSIVELY SO THAT WE HAVE A CHANCE AT ACHIEVING OUR PROFESSIONAL DREAMS . . . HERE AT UW-OSHKOSH. YOU SUGGEST THAT WE CAN ARRANGE IT WITHIN A ONE- OR TWO-YEAR PERIOD TO "FREE-UP" LONGER BLOCKS FOR RESEARCH AND STUDY? BUT WHAT DO WE GAIN BY THIS?

Then comes a conceptual breakthrough. We might be able to meet many of our teaching needs for summer school by releasing faculty from teaching in the spring (after all, spring enrollments are always down). Then we could use a portion of the summer school budget dollars saved in this fashion to "balance the budget." Some will have to teach summer as "part of the load." But the University will be able to protect its tenured faculty. THAT IS AN IMPORTANT DRUID TRADITION. To do this, we will need a new "Calendar" that has more manageable "chunks" of time than seventeen (weeks in a semester), seventeen, and eight. BUT OTHERS HAVE DIFFERENT CALENDARS . . . ISN'T THAT SO?

But the Druids are not easily sold. They know that the long drought has functionally disabled them as entrepreneurs. And they know that they need both time and money to get back on track. WE MAY BE COMPELLED TO SUPPORT THIS

STRANGE NOTION OF TIME MANAGEMENT IF WE CAN GAIN ACCESS TO FUNDING TO PAY US TO PURSUE "DRUID ACTIVITIES."

The faculty are in great difficulty. Aside from extramural grant monies (competitive and difficult to obtain), the only method of earning income to supplement their nine-month salary and support their work lies in teaching summer school. But without adequate support from the University for research, travel, and other professional needs, it is very difficult to successfully live an academic Druid life. Thus, there is great interest in and desperate need for funds to support Druid activities.

Druids are supposed to be entrepreneurs. At UW–Oshkosh, they were turning into intrapreneurs as the last line of defense against their fading dream: a university life devoted to teaching, writing, and professional work (research, artistic productions, music, etc.).

And, by coincidence, Faculty Development was replacing Institutional Research as the "thing to do"throughout higher education. So it was professionally legitimate to use these words . . . at least at this moment in time. WHO KNOWS? MAYBE THIS WILL BECOME A NEW DRUID TRADITION?

As it turned out, yet another part of the solution to the puzzle was unfolding. The "self-pacers" with the support of their Dean had emerged from their experience with an idea to bury the traditional bull-pen registration (held in a large gathering place—usually a gymnasium, with faculty representatives of each department gathered to admit and advise every student into every course to be taught the next semester) with an on-line, continuous, computer-based one. That way students could start and stop school as they wish. ANOTHER STRANGE IDEA . . . BUT DRUIDS NEVER LIKED WORKING IN BULLPEN REGISTRATIONS ANYWAY . . . THAT IS PROPER WORK FOR CLERKS AND COMPUTERS!

Why does the organization tolerate these strange ideas? Perhaps simply because there are no better ones . . . and there simply is little energy to resist. Many do not agree with them, but they do not have the energy to allocate to disagreeing. They are focused on keeping the flickering flame of their professional dreams alive. JUST DO NOT THREATEN MY JOB SE-

CURITY ANY MORE THAN IT ALREADY IS. AND IF YOU MUST CHANGE THE FOREST, DO IT QUICKLY . . . AND THE DRUID GODS BE WITH YOU!

In late spring of 1974 the Chancellor forms a Calendar Study Committee. He charges its members to review the "calendar literature" and recommend the"chunks of time" that will make sense for UW–Oshkosh. They work into the summer; their discussion provides a legitimate forum for discussion of the University and of managing time. The committee recommends a calendar in which each semester is made up of Three 5's (courses could be five weeks, ten weeks, or fifteen weeks long) and one 2 (one two-week module). The Chancellor rejects it, quietly. This type of pattern is too different from the three-week and four-week courses now taught (in the "interim" between the seventeen-week semesters), and the eight-week summer session (which includes two four-week blocks as an option). It is also too "inflexible" . . . too uniform.

But there are other reasons to resist this notion. The new way of arranging time must be one that permits, but does not *force,* substantial change in the way professors' lecture notes read. Druids will choose to change their teaching but will not be told to do so. The "All 5" plan is far too disruptive. Everyone will have all class/lecture preparations to do completely over at once. The Chancellor is right. The idea cannot be sold to the Druids.

At the same time, the egalitarian streak in the new Chancellor becomes more visible and unsettling. He openly promotes the idea of Open Admissions. He moves easily among students, faculty, and staff. He downplays "Outstanding Teaching Awards," pomp and circumstance at graduations, and symbols of distinction. He brings with him the values of the urban campus. Everyone deserves an opportunity to succeed. These notions make many of the Druids uncomfortable.

But the Chancellor makes up for this by rounding up more little red wagons for his parade. All universities are full of solutions looking for problems to attach themselves to. And each Druid has a unique problem, and sometimes several—new ways to teach, paintings and sculptures to complete, specialized research projects. The ideas and dreams had really collected dur-

ing the long professional drought. The Chancellor invites them
all to join his parade. In 1974 UW–Oshkosh submits *twelve* proposals to the Fund for the Improvement of Post-secondary Education. TWELVE!! A SIGN OF RENEWED INTEREST IN WHO
WE ARE AND WHAT WE DO. The changes at the University
are picking up steam, twelve proposals is hyperactivity! From
UW–Zero! Two eventually are funded.

So, during the summer of 1974 the professionally starved
Druids began to emerge from their forests with their shaken
dreams and "joined the parade." Their professional spirit was
rekindled. The summer is spent by the Chancellor, UW System
administrators, and the faculty talking, thinking, and setting
the stage for what will come.

YES, MR. CHANCELLOR, THERE MAY BE A WAY FOR US
TO BE ABLE TO SUPPORT THESE STRANGE TIME MAN-
AGEMENT IDEAS. WHILE THE DRUID TRADITION IS
STRONG, SUMMER IS A TIME FOR DRUID WORK, NOT
TEACHING. WE MAY ALSO BE ABLE TO ACCEPT TEACH-
ING IN THE SUMMER SESSION WITHOUT THE EXTRA PAY
SO MANY OF US (WHO DO TEACH) ARE USED TO RE-
CEIVING. WE MAY EVEN BE ABLE TO ACCEPT THIS
"STRANGE" INSTITUTIONAL IDENTITY . . . AND THE IDEA
OF OPEN ADMISSION . . . AND THE OTHER IDEAS YOU
HAVE THAT ARE NOT PART OF OUR TRADITION. CON-
SIDER TAKING SOME OF THE MONEY YOU SAY WE WILL
SAVE BY MAKING THESE CHANGES AND USING IT TO SET
UP A REALLY SUBSTANTIAL FUND TO SUPPORT OUR
DRUID WAYS.

The Druids had become intrapreneurs!

At other points in time and space, this type of an ideological
trade-off might not have worked. But the stakes were very high
here . . . and they were high in a variety of quarters. They
were high for the Druids, because for many this was probably
their last chance to hope to see a restored forest at Oshkosh. If
this failed they would have to leave to pursue their Druidism.
They were high for the Chancellor, as this was his best chance
to see if his best idea (managing time) would work. They were
high for several of the Chancellor's sponsors in the UW System
Administration. The visibly severe budget problem at UW–

Oshkosh, one that seemed at times impossible to deal with realistically, was compromising tough decisions in every imaginable area with the other universities in the recently merged (and still fragile) UW System. And the stakes were high for the Board of Regents, because any "troubled campus" represents a problem that it must deal with in a politically acceptable manner.

And all constituencies had to support "the deal," UW System especially so for many reasons. A new Calendar would contaminate the "clean" student credit hour and faculty workload data that were now being collected in UW System computers. (All other campuses counted students on the 10th day of Fall classes and these student credit hours drove budget for the next year. At Oshkosh the numbers would be different; the UW System management information systems [and budgeting mechanisms] would be affected.) And if you were going to ask faculty to teach summer as "part of load," new payroll and contract flexibility would be required, that, in effect, would permit faculty to be paid on August 1 for work that they might not perform until September or October. And that was very close to a violation of a state statute. These are only a few of the many administrative hurdles that had to be overcome for the deal to "stick."

Those who were able to stand back from the individual problems and look at the set saw that one problem often became another problem's solution. UW System needed some visible progress in the Faculty Development arena. Oshkosh had too many tenured faculty, and some on lay-off status. The Druids needed time and money for professional activity. The Chancellor needed the Summer Session taught as part of load. The self-pacers wanted a Continuous Registration system to support their teaching methodology. The students wanted more flexibility in adjusting their work around the academic Calendar. A few students wanted to graduate in less than four "standard" years to reduce the escalating costs of higher education. The Regents wanted us off the "troubled campus" list. INTERESTING. NOW IF WE DO THIS RIGHT, MANY GET MOST OF WHAT THEY WANT. OK. BUNDLE IT UP. LET'S MAKE A DEAL!

But this is a complicated deal . . . although the environment is *not* supportive of risk taking. Many are scared. Most are completely discouraged. Nearly all are disoriented. Given these conditions, how do you build a coalition of understanding to move the organization through a change of this magnitude? How do you create real understanding of this pack of maneuvers?

At last there is a visible outcome of the spring and summer efforts. The Chancellor begins to write a series of "Calendar Papers." In late August 1974, the first one emerges. The concepts are taken in order. One deals with the demographic reality. He enlists the help of several competent Druids to do the projections . . . the right way. They have been working over the summer. Other Druids help with papers on faculty contracting patterns. One paper deals with Faculty Development. There are thirteen papers in all, and they flow out into the campus community over a period of fifty days! They are comprehensive, and often complicated. Some of them are read. All are discussed. These writings are the "old testament" for the culture-to-come. They create a vision of how things will be when the promise is kept.

One Calendar Paper (Number 3) is a response to the Calendar Committee. It is distributed early in the Fall semester of 1974. The Chancellor "plops" *the* decision on the organization. He proposes that we adopt a 4–4 (two four-week summer sessions), 7 week–7 week–3 week, 7–7–3, academic Calendar. AT LEAST THAT ADDS UP RIGHT. 7 + 7 + 3 = 17 WEEKS. And our Summer Session has been taught in two 4's for years. INTERESTING! 4–4–773–773. IS THAT ANYONE'S SOCIAL SECURITY NUMBER? NO, IT HAS TOO FEW DIGITS. Someone has a shirt printed with 44–773–773 and gives it to the Chancellor. He laughs. He wears it.

Another Calendar Paper deals with money to support the Druid ways. There must be sacrifice by the individual faculty if the entire faculty is to gain. Faculty who are paid for summer teaching will be paid at a rate of 7.5 percent of their base salary per course (rather than 11 percent): the maximum that can be earned will be 15 percent (rather than 22 percent). But support will be available to more faculty because, of the $500,000 to be spent for "Compensation For Additional Service," $200,000 will be used to support research, curriculum, and other Druid work. This is what the Chancellor promises. It is to be part of the deal.

The selling is not restricted to this highly rational approach. It also proceeds at a personal and social level. The Chancellor visits department meetings, and makes the pitch. There is a round of cocktail dinner parties at the Chancellor's residence, and the invitation lists are carefully screened. There is serious business to be done here. The coalitions are being formed. Special understandings are reached and fine interpretations made. The collective vision is spun, as fragile as a spider's web.

In October of 1974 the last "Calendar Paper" emerges. It calls for a faculty referendum. The decision has to be all or nothing. Some argue that we should consider each idea (new semester system, faculty development, on-line registration, etc.) in turn. No, the Chancellor will not go along with that. It is all or nothing—Black or White. The deal must remain intact. His integrity is at stake; he means what he has said to all of the groups with whom he has worked. It must be all or nothing.

In late October 1974, the Druids emerge from their forests in large numbers to join the remainder of the faculty and professional staff in the referendum vote. It passes by a substantial margin. The "Calendar Papers" are ratified. *It is less than nine months since the new Chancellor arrived!* But we are not done. The faculty has approved implementation of the changes; it has not approved them as a permanent part of the University. In the spring of 1977 there will be a second referendum in which the changes will be either approved or voted down. We have just over two years to make this thing work. We have *only* one chance!

And as 1974 edges toward the end of the year, the moves accelerate in number. A black administrator (the Chancellor's first appointment, and the first senior-level black administrator at the University—ever) comes on board from Madison in a staff position to the Chancellor. Academic Development (THIS IS A NEW IDEA, AND WE DO NOT UNDERSTAND IT) is his role. Two search committees produce a new Vice Chancellor and a new Graduate Dean. Both will begin near the end of 1974. These are important administrative positions to the Druids.

It is now December 1974. The exact dates of classes, vacations, and commencements in the new Calendar for the 1975–76 year are announced. We are to begin implementing "the Calendar Papers" with the beginning of the 1975 Summer Session. The students will preregister for the Fall Semester, 1975, in April. The academic schedule must be set in March. The Druids expect resources for their professional work to be available in June. There are many questions and issues to be settled. Time is very short.

Yet even the hectic pace does not permit decisions that extend the effects of the Calendar Plan beyond the bounds of "The Deal." The Chancellor wants to "tweak" the academic Calendar by scheduling the traditional Easter-week break in a time in March so that the University is not in session during the week of the "St Pat's bash at Oshkosh." No matter the merit of his arguments, he does not prevail. His political capital is spent. It was not part of the change package approved in the referendum.

As Christmas approaches, the second wave of key personnel changes in the organization takes place. A key fiscal officer (one with independent connections to UW System administration, and who did not fully support the new Chancellor's ideas) returns to the classroom. He is replaced by a staffer (previously a nonfaculty staff person for the past and current Chancellor) who had been a key contact with the "Druid clans" on the campus. One of the "Druid leaders" is appointed to a key academic support position in the (now vacant, but soon to be filled) Vice Chancellor's office, and assumes responsibility for the key technical support units needed for the Calendar to be implemented (Admissions, Registration and Records, Data Processing). These changes were announced simultaneously and suddenly. The Chancellor's implementation plan begins. Time is very short indeed.

Thank goodness that the "Techies" (computer services personnel who work in data processing) were ready; they had guessed right. They had been watching the campus debate closely (sometimes asked their opinion, but rarely listened to) and they had kept their ears to the ground. They had considered their options and begun operating on the assumption that the decision would be to implement the new Calendar before half of the Calendar Papers had even been written. They have already begun the massive design and development work needed to support student registration, records, and accounting under the new Calendar. And they have done this without the blessings of the senior administrator (one of the second-wave casualties) to whom they have reported. But now they report to a Druid, and they can go public with their needs for decisions and technology. They are now out in the open and visibly part of the effort to preserve the forest.

Here the organization gets lucky—maybe dumb lucky. We have not really fully estimated just how difficult it will be to redesign and reequip our information systems to handle this "real-time" Calendar. Under normal circumstances, the lack of technical resources in a time of tight budgets would strangle the development effort. But the technical units have considerable "slack" available (both machine and personnel resources) to reallocate to this effort because overall management of this function has been poor (a common feature of universities in the mid-70s). IF WE CAN ONLY LEARN TO MANAGE THESE RESOURCES CORRECTLY, WE CAN MAKE IT HAPPEN WITHOUT SPENDING THE EXTRA DOLLARS THAT WE SIMPLY DO NOT HAVE. The organization learns quickly.

As 1975 unfolds, the magnitude of what is being attempted is just setting in. Virtually every facet of the University will feel the changes, and these changes are coming on the organization very quickly. FOR SURE, WE HAVE BEEN GIVEN THE AUTHORITY AND OPPORTUNITY TO RESTORE THE FOREST, BUT WE MUST DO IT QUICKLY . . . VERY QUICKLY.

Two major fronts are opened. In one, a "Kleenex committee" (disposable and thrown away when used) called the Calendar Steering Committee is formed. It meets weekly, and contains a mixture of faculty and administrators, some old hands and some new ones. It has fourteen subcommittees (each chaired by a member of the Steering Committee and involving seven to ten individuals not on the Committee), each of which focuses on a specific problem or program associated with implementing the new concepts. There is one for fiscal considerations, another for Academic Standards. But one, above all, is key to the Druids. That is the Faculty Development Program Committee.

This group (all Druids, hand-picked by the Chancellor) is given the task of creating the policies and procedures that are to govern the allocation of funds to get the professional lifeblood of the University running again. This is the time for Druids to become visible, because there are *good* decisions to make, decisions about how scarce internal resources are to be allocated to prime the professional pumps, not decisions identifying who gets laid off.

But there are few precedents to follow. Most Faculty Development programs in other universities are administrative shells . . . Faculty Development Specialists, Teaching Excellence Centers, and the like. This is not the stuff of Druids!

The dominant Faculty Development Committee culture is that of scientists. The National Science Foundation incentive grant model becomes the prototype for decision-making. Druids will prepare proposals, and they will be reviewed by Druid peers, with the highest scores winning the resource prizes. Are the Deans to be involved? NO, NOT UNLESS THEY ARE PROFESSIONALLY QUALIFIED TO ACT AS JURORS FOR A PROPOSAL. Expert power prevails over legitimate power. That is, after all, the Druid way.

Some skeptics outside the committee say, "Why bother? The program will fail, and if it does not, the funding for it (which, in large measure, comes from shifting contracts so that summer session is taught as "part of load") will soon dry up. True, revitalizing the professional spirit of the University faculty is a noble cause. But more powerful claims for these public tax dollars will soon emerge. We will never be more than a high school with ashtrays."

As the Faculty Development Program takes form through the early months of 1975, it becomes a major vehicle for the continuing coalition-building effort. The Druid committee presses on. A pact has been made . . . and the Druids will deliver on their end of the bargain. The Druid committee meets three times a week, rationalizing, writing, arguing, rewriting. In only three weeks, it unanimously passes on the policies and procedures document for the Research Component of the Faculty Development Program. And only two weeks later, it passes on the Curriculum Development Component to support the development of courses using new teaching methods adapted to new time frames and new student audiences. Control over this component had been privately promised to the Deans by the Chancellor in the prereferendum lobbying, with an understanding that (1) this program component would be the largest in the Faculty Development Program and (2) the Deans would have a major role in the allocation of those funds.

The Druid Committee does not deliver for the Chancellor on the second provision. WE UNDERSTAND, BUT THAT IS TOO BAD. WE WERE NOT PART OF THAT DEAL. AND ANYWAY, THE DRUID WAY IS TO HAVE EXPERTS DECIDE ON THE MERITS OF PROPOSALS, NOT ADMINISTRATORS.

These two incentive grant programs (research and curriculum) will divert nearly 2 percent of the University's tax- and tuition-provided budget into the Druid community, to support Druid activities. There is no program more abundantly funded in the country!

How does it happen so quickly? It must. It is a highly rational set of policies and procedures. Politics is out. Being expert is in. Who you know is out. Being a Druid is in. These documents are reviewed and passed on by the Calendar Steering Committee. The Chancellor asks why the Academic Deans are not given more authority to allocate curriculum development resources on the basis of their legitimate power. WE CHOOSE NOT TO HAVE THEM MORE INVOLVED. AGAIN, IT IS NOT THE DRUID WAY. That answer sticks. The Druids risk ignoring the Chancellor's considerable referent power.

These documents also must be considered and ratified by the Faculty Senate. This is a political arena, not a rational one. Surely its members will amend, append, and generally worry the program to death. But they do not. The proposals pass through untouched, and quickly. In spite of the fact that faculty senates are not often attended by Druids, there are some influential Druids on the Senate. And everyone knows that there has been an extended professional drought. As one of the Senators says, "We are talking about money, folks . . . money for the faculty.

Let's vote on it now." They do. But they do not really know what they have done.

In early 1975 (now only one year after the new Chancellor first arrived) the incentive grant opportunities of the UW–Oshkosh Faculty Development Program go public. The pent-up demand for resources to nourish the professional lifeblood of the organization produces a flood of proposals: some good and carefully thought out through the lean years in the forest, and some quite obviously hastily assembled. Some of the proposals are clearly opportunistic, motivated by a desire to "get a piece of the action" before this "new money" goes away. The new Faculty Development Board (Druids, one and all) consider, evaluate, and award. REAL MONEY TO SUPPORT OUR DRUID WAYS DURING THE TIMES WE ARE NOT TEACHING. THE CALENDAR PLAN IS REAL. NOW WE MUST PREPARE TO IMPLEMENT THE FALL TEACHING SCHEDULE WITH ITS MODULES OF 7, 7, AND 3 WEEKS. WE MUST ALSO BECOME ACTIVE WITHIN OUR CLANS TO SEE THAT OUR END OF THE "DEAL" IS KEPT.

The Faculty Development (Druid) Committee wrestles with the concept of in-service development programming. A STRANGE NOTION, INDEED. UNIVERSITIES DO NOT HAVE "IN-SERVICE" PROGRAMS FOR DRUIDS. THAT IS AN IDEA FOR HIGH SCHOOLS. The committee finally adopts a neutral name for their program: it will be known as the FACULTY COLLEGE. It will feature instruction for faculty, by faculty . . . on new and interesting professional subjects. What's in a name?

Then, several more pieces to the Faculty Development Program: The Off-Campus program provides opportunities for faculty to obtain full funding (not the partial funding typically awarded by academic administrators with their soup-extender approach) to travel off-campus to structured programs of professional development . . . short courses, visitor programs, participation in workshops, private lessons with musical performers, and so on. THE FULL FUNDING ASPECT OF THIS PROGRAM IS OBVIOUSLY PREFERRED . . . BUT MORE IMPORTANTLY, IT IS NOT PROPER FOR A DRUID TO HAVE TO ASK AN ACADEMIC ADMINISTRATOR FOR A HANDOUT TO TRAVEL TO A LEGITIMATE DRUID ACTIVITY. THIS

IS GOOD. DRUIDS ARE ONLY USING WHAT IS RIGHT-FULLY THEIRS!

Still, there are others who have projects that do not fit neatly into the expanding array of program components. Several Druids on the Chancellor's "kitchen cabinet" suggest that support be given for the implementation of their ideas on how the University environment should evolve. The Druid committee responds. Funding is made available for sculptures to be constructed. General Education issues are to be studied. Faculty are to be surveyed on issues related to faculty governance.

These later program components emerge quickly. And some gain wide support. They serve as vehicles through which all can gain something from the new program. They serve to expand the dominant coalition. Participation begets support for the new ideas. More Druids are seen emerging from the deep forests. Some faculty who were never Druids are becoming Druids. That is what development is all about.

In March of 1975, the Chancellor announces that the Calendar subcommittee for Faculty Development (among others) is disbanding, its work being over. Later in that same month, the selection process for the first Faculty Development Board (which will oversee the implementation of the program that the earlier Druid Committee had structured) is completed. Again, the members of this group are Druids, one and all. The expert-respecting Druids are thus seen as also being capable of political action. It is unusual for Druid Faculty to be so involved with "politics." But here they are given an opportunity to maintain their values and beliefs. They participate.

Through these times, the legitimate power structure of the academic administration is faced with a series of challenges. A new, vigorous Vice Chancellor has taken up office and begins to lead. He challenges the Deans to recover some of the decision-making authority that has been dispersed to others and taken from them in the chaos of previous years. He also challenges them to be vigorous in the pursuit of the goals of the Chancellor's Calendar Plan (one that they did not generally support prior to the referendum). These conditions lead, within a short time, to a change of guard in a majority of the deanships.

These moves, and several key staff appointments by the Chancellor, solidify the Chancellor's hold on the decision-making structures of the organization. In each change, the Druids are carefully consulted. And after each, the Druids can be more frequently seen in the professional plains surrounding their forest glens.

On the technical side of the organization, there is a frantic (often desperate) push to completely rethink how information is handled to support the "continuous activity" aspect of the new Calendar. The proponents of individualized instruction have recognized that the student registration and grade-reporting functions need to move from "batch" to "real-time" mode in order for self-pacing to work. They have not, however, fully appreciated the second- and third-level effects that this change will have on student records, student accounts, and financial aid. And the demands that the flexible contracting and teaching workloads were to place on systems to support the faculty and staff personnel/payroll function are still to be perceived.

And so the technology of "Continuous Registration" is born. Away with the "bullpen" registration sessions that consumed most of a week. We will do it at terminals, each day, all year long. After all, the airlines have managed to implement a similar scheduling system, haven't they? The ideas are simple: Create a schedule of courses, each with a fixed seat capacity, each with a "teacher-pilot," and each with a start and stop date. Then let students plan their "academic itineraries," come to the "scheduling center," and see if they can "make the connection." If seats are available, print an invoice. It's done.

Not quite. It is a new design, and a new technology. Virtually no one has sensed the magnitude of the redistribution of power that this represents . . . power related to the relationships between academic administrators, faculty, and students. The more alert of the faculty quickly begin to negotiate over *both* the content and the timing of their teaching schedules . . . and these complexities weaken the positions of academic department heads and deans. The students negotiate with virtually no one . . . they go to the scheduling center and simply enroll in available courses . . . by talking with a sympathetic terminal operator rather than indifferent department office personnel. The University's academic administration can now study the current and projected schedule of offerings with more time and thought, and place additional controls on the class scheduling/balancing process. The concept of actually *managing* the distribution of the collective faculty teaching resource through the year begins to emerge.

The summer of 1975 is very hectic. The concepts are new, the issues are deep, and time is short. There are virtually no precedents . . . anywhere. Here, one must depend on being expert, energetic, and lucky. Continuing students need to schedule and preregister for the fall. The software to support the continuous concepts of the Calendar is still under development. But the students need to register for the Fall semester . . . NOW! So we improvise. We do whatever we need to do to get the job done. In jest, one Druid wag observes that "Nothing motivates action like sheer terror!" Most smile, some do not. There is more to this observation than many who hear it think!

The ten months between the referendum and the implementation of the Calendar pass quickly. In September 1975, we find that the technical team has met its challenge and that the student registration system works. (We will not know how many students have actually registered until well into the spring of 1976 . . . because there is no time to write the programs to prepare accurate enrollment reports, but registration works.) We have to leave the student accounts part of the system behind because the accountants cannot define their system within the time available, and so there is some confusion over who owes whom how much and when . . . but here we are protected by the inertia of the state bureaucracy!

Through these months the Public Relations workers in the organization churn mightily—words, symbols, charts, more words. We write about what we are doing so that WE can understand it. And as we write, the images become clearer and clearer. A University of Alternatives. New power to students and faculty . . . to control time. "Students, take control of when you study." The message is simple: "Manage the time demands of your education *and* your part-time job." The message to faculty is equally simple: "Faculty, take control of the time of your professional lives, the time blocks in your contracts. Manage your professional time. Express your ideas to the Faculty Development Board (Druids, one and all) and use the resources that are *yours* to regain your rightful position in the larger professional community." WE HEAR YOU. WE ARE CATCHING ON. THIS IS A BIT STRANGE, THIS GOING TO THE ORGANIZATION FOR RESOURCES TO SUPPORT OUR DRUID WAYS. BUT PERHAPS WE ARE DIFFEENT HERE AT OSHKOSH?

There is a very great deal to do . . . and a very great many lend a hand. The activity draws ever-increasing numbers of the Druids out of the deep forests. The commotion (noted even in the *New York Times*) also begins to attract to Oshkosh new academic administrators from other organizations, individuals with the self-confidence to embrace strange ideas and demanding environments. The blend of power in the organization is changing quickly. It has moved well into the domain of the expert. If you know, and can effectively implement, people listen. Who you are, and what title you hold is of lesser importance. And who you know, and which political group you are identified with, is of little importance. There is simply too much to do . . . and too few to do it. Being expert is in.

We had started the change process only two years prior. It is now January 1976. There are key indicators to watch . . . the most prominent being the final Fall 1975 Semester Enrollment, which will not be known until the end of the three-week post-Christmas term. IS IT MORE SECURE HERE AT THE FOREST FRINGE, WHERE WE MAY BE AT RISK, THAN DEEP IN THE FOREST? And then the good news. The long decline in Fall Semester enrollments is reversed! Indeed there is some confusion over what the numbers mean, now that students come and go much more easily . . . and our sister universities are challenging these new numbers, since our new success weakens their bargaining position for our resources. But with the help of our sponsors in UW System Administration, we prevail. The long, disastrous Oshkosh enrollment decline is generally agreed to be broken. Still, some of the Druids remain deep in the forest. PERHAPS THE ACTIVITY IS MAKING THE ENVIRONMENT BETTER FOR OUR WAYS . . . BUT THESE NEW WAYS ARE TOO STRANGE.

What do the students think? They have adapted quickly (the young always do) and they like it. Every survey confirms this. Why? The new Calendar and continuous registration help them obtain and schedule summer and vacation jobs. The new Calendar gives them new choices for class lengths, even though many do not take them. And registration is easier . . . much easier. So why would anyone want to go back to the old ways? Indeed, many do not even remember the old ways . . . and with each passing semester, more have never experienced them.

1976 passes quickly. It is a year of refining, consolidating, and fixing. Through it all, the institutional researchers are surveying *everything*. This is done to satisfy the rational dimension of the University, and to give our sponsors the means to rationalize their continued support. These sponsors need numbers. The surveys continue to tell us that, as far as the Calendar, registration, and the students are concerned, the new is better than the old . . . perhaps not as much as we might have hoped, but perceptibly better.

New sponsors are found. Representatives of the prestigious Lilly Endowment visit the campus to determine if they will lend their hand to the Faculty Development program. They speak with a wide variety of individuals in private. Is this real? Can this really work? Are the Druids really in control of their professional destinies? They decide that the answer is *yes* to all questions. A substantial amount of badly needed funding is awarded to help cement the Faculty Development Program in place. The Fund for the Improvement of Post Secondary Education awards a series of major grants to Calendar-related activities. Activity levels rise. WHILE IT IS TIRING, IT IS ALSO FUN . . . AT LEAST MOST OF IT IS!

So, suggestions that we return to the old ways cannot be sustained. The risks of returning to the deep forest are much higher than the risks of staying at the forest fringe. And, anyway, who will mobilize the very great amount of energy needed to make the reverse change? Change registration, and the underlying software systems that support the new concepts?

Change back to inflexible faculty contracts? Take away our opportunities for professional development even if we can get paid a little more to teach summer school? Make it harder for students to "step out" temporarily in order to make money to pay tuition? SURELY YOU JEST!

The stream of visitors often seems to be unending! They come from other universities where the Druids are also retreating deep in the forest. Most often, the visitors are fascinated, and they spend several days to understand the *whole* thing. It is clear to all that one cannot do this in pieces. It is all or nothing. They have never seen anything like *this*! Can the idea be transplanted? "Not the whole thing . . . that will be impossible. Maybe a piece of it . . . and maybe we can do it slowly." The Druids smile quietly. THE VISITORS WILL NEVER BE ABLE TO DO IT. A DEAL IS A DEAL.

In February of 1977 the Chancellor distributes a report on Calendar Reform. In a series of graphs and tables, he reports that University enrollments are substantially above projections, many more faculty are receiving additional funds (beyond their base academic year contract) than in previous years, nearly 20 percent of the faculty have adopted "nontraditional" time patterns for meeting their contractual obligations, and that the UW–Oshkosh has (in only two years) catapulted from seventh to first (among its peers in the UW System) as measured by the receipt of extramural funds. THE LATTER IS A GENUINE MEASURE OF OUR (DRUID) PROGRESS.

Early in the spring of 1977, the second referendum on the whole "program" (Calendar, Faculty Development, etc.) is held. As in the Fall of 1974, it is an "all or nothing" choice. SHALL WE CONTINUE IN THESE NEW WAYS, OR SHALL WE RETREAT TO THE "BEFORE TIME?" IT IS NOT QUITE AS SOME HAD DREAMED. YET WE SEEM TO BE ADAPTING, AND THE FOREST EDGE SEEMS TO HAVE STABILIZED. AND THERE IS STILL NO BETTER IDEA. The second referendum passes on a close vote (234–204). A wag observes that "More would have voted against it but they were afraid that the referendum might not pass." VERY TRUE! The Druid population is growing.

Yet despite a growing faith that UW–Oshkosh could become

something, despite a growth in number of Druid faculty, and despite three years of intensive change work with a backdrop of fiscal crisis and the greatest threat to faculty imaginable (tenure layoffs!) the changes pass by a scant thirty votes! But they pass.

It is late Spring 1977. The sense of immediate danger is a distant memory. What was new is now nearly routine. Symbols such as Faculty College, two-year contracts for faculty, three-week courses, internally funded grants for research, curriculum development, support for extended periods of (expensive) off-campus activity . . . IT SEEMS NATURAL THAT THINGS BE THIS WAY. SURELY OTHER DRUID CIVILIZATIONS HAVE THESE THINGS! But they do not. The Druids do not perceive how different they have become.

One of the extramural grants awarded to the University in 1975 was to sponsor a formal study of the "Oshkosh Calendar Plan" to determine its effectiveness in achieving the vision that was cast in the "Calendar Papers" that preceded the first referendum. As the final report for that study (delivered in 1977) put it, in seeking to enhance faculty development:

Without doubt, this . . . goal and its accomplishment are the jewel of the innovation. By hard data and by testimony, faculty development has been an outstanding success. . . . What makes its accomplishment all the more salutary is that its continual accomplishment is built right into the innovation. FD [Faculty Development] at UW–Oshkosh is not a one-shot affair, a sky rocket that will obliterate itself when the first flash is over; rather . . . [it] is a regular and ongoing feature of the calendar reform, a bright satellite permanently in orbit. (Blackburn, 1977, pp. 72–73)

So it is done. And while the smoke still lingers at the forest fringe, the fire fighters are packing up and preparing to leave. The forest is safe and the Durids are observed more frequently exercising their traditional professional rites in the sunlight. They are again hard at it, and the lifeblood of the University is flowing again . . . from hundreds of individual professional pumphearts. A new changeover in the legitimate power structure of the organization has begun. As the ideas in Calendar Reform are better understood, they lose their fascination. Those who have been drawn to them seek other ideas to develop, in other places.

So too, the Chancellor prepares to leave. His spirit also needs renewal. He correctly views being a Chancellor as a role, not a career. The University *has* changed under his leadership. But if the Druids are to truly adopt the new ways into their traditions, he must leave.

Interestingly, he seeks a forest clan that he can join as a Druid. Some will be glad to see him go. Some of those actively engaged in the contest have lost. For others who have refrained from the foray, the din on the forest fringe has been very distracting. Some, however, will miss him. I WONDER . . . COULD AN IDEA-SET OF THIS MAGNITUDE HAVE BEEN PUT IN PLACE BY OTHER THAN A DRUID?

The Fisher-King has fallen sick and, in typical Celtic fashion, his illness affects the entire environment. Towers crumble, gardens wilt, animals cease to breed, the springs no longer flow, there is no fruit on the trees. Every attempt is made to find a cure. All fail, until a young knight called Parsifal [probably, the Peredur of the early Welsh tales] burst in among the courtiers. He asks one question: Where is the Grail? The question is enough. The king rises from his bed and the dying world around him reawakens.

'The world is perishing,' says Eliade, 'because of . . . metaphysical indifference.' The mere asking of the question is enough to show that indifference is gone. (Rutherford, 1978, p. 155)

POSTSCRIPT

The new Calendar, with its two semesters of two seven-week and one three-week term, and its summer session of two four-week terms, provided much greater flexibility for faculty and student course scheduling. In addition, by extending the class period from fifty to sixty minutes, it became possible to teach a standard load of twelve credits in fourteen weeks rather than seventeen. This permitted faculty members to teach for fourteen weeks and then have three weeks for research (or teach fifteen credits in seventeen weeks), work patterns not possible under the traditional calendar.

As part of the same broad series of reforms, the University adopted the concept of the annual contract. The Calendar enabled faculty members to schedule blocks of time during the year to accommodate their own personal and professional development plans. The obligation of a faculty member was unchanged (i.e., to teach twenty-four credits and participate in University service for thirty-four weeks each year). While the inclusion of summer teaching as part of regular load was theoretically possible under the old calendar and contract provisions, it would have taken "Stalinist" tactics to gain faculty acceptance of the loss of extra teaching compensation and the prospect of being tied to campus for both semesters and the summer unless meaningful incentives could be offered. These incentives were created by the two other changes, the flexibility of the new Calendar and the Faculty Development Program.

In 1974 all 214 summer faculty members teaching summer school had received extra compensation. In the 1975 summer session, when the annual-load contract was initiated, of the 205 faculty members teaching in that session, 80 taught courses as part of their annual regular load. The savings from 1974 to 1975 from this strategy alone was $225,000. During 1975–76, nearly 20 percent of the faculty chose scheduling plans featuring teaching summer session as part-of-load and involving some time off during the "regular" academic year. This pattern of use continues.

A major portion of the money saved from the change in summer session staffing was reinvested in the organization in the form of the Faculty Development Program. The Faculty Development Program allows faculty to receive up to 15 percent of their academic-year salaries as "Compensation for Additional Service" (CAS). Awards in the research and curricular areas are competitive, made by and administered through a Faculty Development Board comprised of faculty peers. The Faculty College is a constantly changing series of short courses for faculty members conducted by other faculty members and outside guests. During 1975–76, 95 research/curriculum de-

velopment proposals were supported and 189 faculty members were enrolled in ten one-week programs during the three-week January term. The number of faculty seeking and receiving Faculty Development support has continued.

This investment enabled the University to improve its curriculum and the capabilities of its faculty (and generally to increase the "carrying capacity" of the organization). The level of fiscal support is substantially higher today.

The unique characteristic of this innovation was that it linked an increase in staff productivity to a professional development incentive system within the framework of a flexible academic Calendar.

To this day, all of the major aspects of the innovation, including the comprehensive Faculty Development Program, continue to function as originally described within the thirteen Calendar Papers.

PART IV

UNDERSTANDING

Chapter 9
Understanding the Intrapreneurship

What does the process of intrapreneurship look like? Can we conceptualize intrapreneurship in such a way that we can, in one place, present it to the reader in its entirety? We think so. Scientists use models to interpret observations. The model presented herein provides the dimensions and variables which must be accounted for in any intrapreneurial work. (See Figure 2.) Some of the organizational processes depicted and variables listed will require no change in an institution; others will have to be modified if the intrapreneurs' work is to succeed. By use of the model, intrapreneurs should be better able to conceptualize their game plans both before and during their intrapreneurial work.

To clarify academic intrapreneurship, we will apply the model to the intrapreneurs' work described in Chapter 8. Ours is a case study and we believe it is representative of how academic intrapreneurship can proceed. But the work at our University is only one scenario out of many in the world of academic change and intrapreneurship.

A word of caution is in order. While our model of intrapreneurship assists in clarifying a very complex process, there is the danger of oversimplification. We agree with Kanter (1983a) that paradoxes are reality. There is no singular formula for change. If, in applying the model of intrapreneurship, the Ex-

Figure 2
A Model of Intrapreneurship

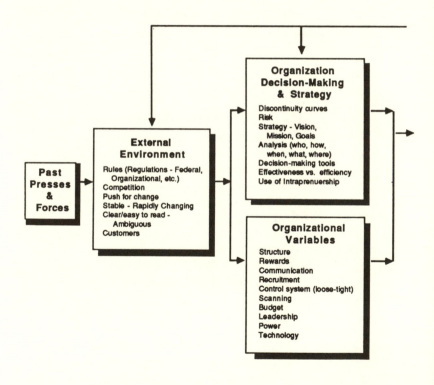

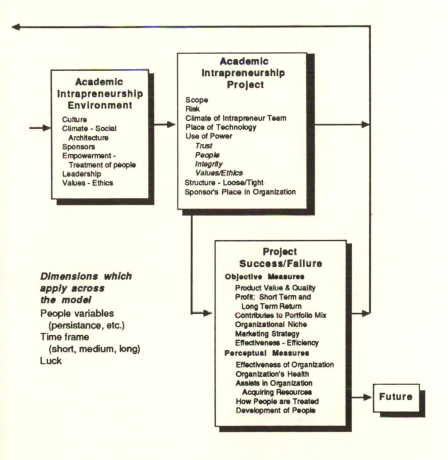

Academic Intrapreneurship Environment

Culture
Climate - Social
   Architecture
Sponsors
Empowerment -
   Treatment of people
Leadership
Values - Ethics

Academic Intrapreneurship Project

Scope
Risk
Climate of Intrapreneur Team
Place of Technology
Use of Power
   Trust
   People
   Integrity
   Values/Ethics
Structure - Loose/Tight
Sponsor's Place in Organization

Dimensions which apply across the model
People variables
   (persistance, etc.)
Time frame
   (short, medium, long)
Luck

Project Success/Failure

Objective Measures

   Product Value & Quality
   Profit: Short Term and
      Long Term Return
   Contributes to Portfolio Mix
   Organizational Niche
   Marketing Strategy
   Effectiveness - Efficiency

Perceptual Measures

   Effectiveness of Organization
   Organization's Health
   Assists in Organization
      Acquiring Resources
   How People are Treated
   Development of People

Future

107

ternal Environment seemed to drive change in an organization, a closer inspection will show that people had an important role. If, in inspecting an Innovation Project, a group seemed to act, there were strong individuals (e.g., mentors and sponsors) who worked hard. Conversely, if single actors seem important, look for an acting troupe. If recent events seem prominent, take a close look at Past Presses and Forces. If, in assessing the Organization Decision-Making and Strategy or the Academic Intrapreneurship Environment, consensus seemed easily won, look for disagreements and bargaining. If there seems to be an ultimate, clear-sighted strategic or intrapreneurial choice, beware of many small choices along the way. For example, in the intrapreneurship we described, what may appear to be clear-sighted strategy sprang partly from luck and accident.

Finally, in considering the Future, an innovation which seems to last forever may be in trouble. The strong can be fragile.

It is our hypothesis that the structure and content of the intrapreneurship process is the same for academic institutions, other third-sector institutions (nonprofit and nongovernment organizations), and private for-profit corporations alike. Academic institutions can change, can move rapidly, and can utilize current organizational theory and behavior concepts when they must.

The model of intrapreneurship reads from left (Past Presses and Forces) to right (The Future). In actuality, the process of intrapreneurship is interactive, with all of its major domains influencing each other. This is true because the institutional environment permits action, and actions affect the environment. Intrapreneurial efforts take time. When one is engaged in the process of intrapreneurship, one deals with the entire spectrum, all of the time. The lines with arrows in the model highlight where we believe the most direct and observable relationships of interaction and effect occur.

PAST PRESSES AND FORCES

Intrapreneurship begins with a consideration of Past Presses and Forces, which are an initial and important influence on the organization's External Environment and the organization itself. The intrapreneur must not underestimate the power of the past.

Oshkosh, like many regional universities, grew from a small, adequate teacher's college into a regional university replete with students, buildings, and faculty. Since it had not developed as a collegiate-level institution, it was different from established universities. It suffered from an identity crisis (Sagen and Harcleroad, 1970) and lacked tradition, processes, and experience to assist it with its problems.

In 1974 the organization was 103 years old, yet there were no positive symbols that were Oshkosh! The stories told were mostly about how Oshkosh had been, in a negative sense. Organizational myth had it that the Vice Chancellor used to walk the halls to make sure all male faculty were wearing white shirts and ties (apocryphal or not, the story captured the University's past). Other true stories of faculty receiving tenure and promotion without even applying spoke to the informal, noncompetitive, nonmeritocracy that was Oshkosh. The organization's past was no longer a productive factor in its present. This was reflected in the University's worsening relationship with its external environment.

EXTERNAL ENVIRONMENT

During the 1960s, students flocked to the University. This was probably more the result of demographics than for any other reason (there were more college-age students than ever before and they had to find a seat, somewhere, many to avoid the Vietnam experience). As the University grew, a more complex and then strained relationship with the local community and service region arose. The University's numerous constituencies all sought to shape the institution according to their own images. The turbulence of the times was detrimental to the established institution but probably healthy in the longer term.

Unfortunately, the decline in student enrollment in the early 1970s was not foreseen. The University paid the price for inadequate efficiency and a System Administration inexperienced in the prediction of demographic changes. The result of the faulty enrollment predictions was severe at Oshkosh: budget and tenured faculty were cut.

The most visible goal of the University's intrapreneurship effort would be to move the Organization's Decision-Making and Strategy and the Organizational Variables into a more congruent position with the External Environment. The University had to attract more students (become more competitive); it had to maintain its budget (remain competitive with sister institutions); and it had to respond to external pressures for change. It had to accomplish these changes while either conforming to UW System Administration rules or by getting rules changed (for example, altering the process for counting and reporting student enrollment). The External Environment was changing (enrollment was declining, students were attending college elsewhere) but it was an easy environment to read.

ORGANIZATION DECISION-MAKING AND STRATEGY

Prior to 1974 there had been no formal planning, no emphasis on opportunity, no risks taken, and obviously no use of intrapreneurship. The institution reacted to what was thrust upon it by UW System Administration, by the external environment, and especially by the choices eighteen-year-old individuals made with their parents about where to attend college. The University had no discernible unique function (no market niche) and its mission was murky. "When the pressures are in charge the present gets attention not the future; . . . and political and psychological infighting rules, not meeting the outside needs, threats, and opportunities" (Keller, 1983, p. 75). This typifies a Reactor organization; it was (is) a poor strategy.

The University paid the price for inadequate effectiveness. Status quo behavior had always worked; this seemed to be the strategy of choice. If there was a mechanism for change it was the bandwagon syndrome: If it was popular nationally, give it a try. So we tried self-paced classes, television classes, and a "new" general education curriculum. From a technological perspective, one might say that we always seemed to adopt an innovation about the time that everyone else was leaving it for another. We were always getting on an S-curve when everyone

else was getting off! The University's reputation and enrollment were falling.

ORGANIZATIONAL VARIABLES

Prior to intrapreneurship, these variables had been traditional and well established, solidly anchored in the institution's
past, although not terribly effective. The organization's structure was that of a traditional, process-oriented bureaucracy.
Rewards were not (always) contingent on meritorious behavior
and much such behavior went unrewarded. Communication was
limited, closed, and top-down. Recruitment of faculty was ongoing even with tenure layoffs. The control system, as noted
in Chapter 7, was extremely tight. Scanning of the environment, both internal to the organization and external, was weak,
ineffective, and reactive. Budget was falling. There was a leadership vacuum in the institution. Competition for power existed among upper management and the academic deans. There
was no empowerment. Technology was used in a reactive way
and not effectively.

ACADEMIC INTRAPRENEURSHIP ENVIRONMENT

The UW System Regents wanted a change agent as the
Chancellor at Oshkosh. This was an unusual selection criterion
in the state system. The organization lacked experience with
intrapreneurship and lacked the environment to nurture the
process. One of the Chancellor's major efforts was to remake
this environment so that it could support intrapreneurial work.
To accomplish this, the culture would have to be changed to
better meet the challenges and problems of the institution's internal and external environments.

The new Chancellor quickly assessed the organization. He
began change efforts immediately. The Chancellor had to get
on with the change; he could not risk being bottled up in the
status quo past. This is why formal analysis and deliberate,
time-consuming decision-making had to be avoided. (He was
at the University for four and one-half years. He was not an

intrapreneur who would overstay his welcome, nor one who wanted to manage the changes he had instituted.)

In our case the Academic Intrapreneurship Environment was the "Calendar Plan." Within this plan were seeds for an innovative curriculum and better uses of time management (both organizational and personal). These were presented under the vision of "The University of Alternatives." It was within this vision that the institution's past would be counteracted and the future embraced.

The University of Alternatives was the Chancellor's attempt to remake the institution's environment and galvanize others into helping with its problems. He needed the creativity of those in the organization. This vision reflected the Chancellor's egalitarianism. One important outcome of the Calendar work would be to bring students back to Oshkosh. The University was communicating that it would be sensitive to the needs of students, any students. There would even be open admission. In the short run, quality was sacrificed to maintain the organization's life.

The idea of a University of Alternatives was important in loosening up the institution. As a strategy or tool, the idea was successful; the Calendar referendum passed. As a goal in and of itself (which it may never have been), it failed.

Innovation is sometimes based on the incongruity (Drucker, 1985a) between reality as it actually is and reality as it is assumed to be or as it "ought to be." This is what happened at UW–O. A stable teachers' college had grown into regional university status. There was no way it could be dying; it had never been dying. But it was! A feeling of gloom and impending doom permeated the institution's climate. This incongruity increased the tensions of the crisis and assisted in developing productive intrapreneurship. The threats and anxieties engendered by tenure and staff layoffs, and budget payback, made it possible to "unfreeze" an organization which had not thawed in many, many years. The University would be forced to become a learning organization.

In our example the sponsor's place in the organization was at the top; he was the chief executive officer. The climate in the intrapreneur's team was positive, supportive, and an exciting one.

The changes the Chancellor fostered were based on an extended search of what was possible in the organization. Lindquist (1978), in talking about academic institutions, says that " . . . the political process of reducing threat to vested interests and complying with existing values means that only small deviations from the status quo are very likely" (p. 80). At Oshkosh the intrapreneur chose to embrace a radical change in the organization. In our case Lindquist was proved wrong.

Empowerment of faculty on the numerous ad hoc Calendar committees was to be one key to the changes. The Chancellor and several key faculty exercised leadership. They became sponsors for those with good ideas who were willing to work hard. The new Chancellor valued processes and people in ways different than before.

By providing faculty with support, resources, and information, they were able to assist the Chancellor in successfully changing the University. Individuals who would act as prime movers were needed, and the Chancellor assembled a critical mass of helpful others. He was able to harness people's time, energy, and commitment, thus increasing the organization's capacity to meet new challenges. The Chancellor needed more than quick decisions; he needed faculty interaction, ideas, and synergy. He offered the faculty an opportunity and one has to be impressed with the faculty's commitment to the University.

Empowerment worked because all of its elements (Bennis and Nanus, 1985) were present in the social architecture of the institution during the intrapreneurship. The organization was moving from a formalistic to a collegial one. No longer were directions from authority figures the bases for decisions. These were replaced by discussion and agreement. Controls moved from formal rules and punishments to group commitments and interpersonal interactions and transactions. Being or knowing someone was no longer central; what one thought, felt, and knew became more important. Relating to others as peers rather than in a hierarchial manner facilitated this.

Faculty felt significant and were engaged in serious acts near the heart of things. They were learning and becoming involved in helping save their University. Their feelings of competency rose. Also present were feelings of family and community.

Everyone was in the mess together and there was a feeling of a common cause and common kinship. Last, there was a sense of fun. It was an exhilarating time.

A second key to changes was the empowerment of students. The Chancellor also made a special effort to relate to student leaders. His dress, mannerisms, and often "cavalier" comments helped. He enlisted the students in the struggle to change the University and he was effective. The modular Calendar allowed students to mix and match their academic needs with their needs to maintain jobs which provided the money to pay for the costs of attending college each semester. It is worth noting that this success occurred years before the present-day concern for the amount of education-related debt many students are forced to incur.

Under the new Calendar, students had many options on how to manage their time and their finances so they could attend college. Students could "jump in and out" of college and their classes more often. They had an extra few days to work at the end of summer because the University had no registration week. They also had an extra week at Christmas time to work because the new Calendar had a shorter semester. They could also take more than the usual number of credits and graduate in less than four years. Finally, they could take three-week interim courses free if they were enrolled as full-time students during the longer semester. The need today for empowerment of students in this fashion is greater than ever!

ACADEMIC INTRAPRENEURSHIP

There are always multiple ways of conceptualizing the intrapreneurs' work. A cultural, Druid perspective is described in detail in Chapter 8 and we return to this metaphor periodically throughout the remainder of the book. The second perspective is a more analytical, businesslike approach as summarized in the "Overview" and "The Intrapreneur's World" sections of the book and emphasized in Figure 2 and Table 1. Compared with the Druid metaphor, Table 1 is more static, without affect, a photograph of intrapreneurship frozen in time. It is a very different description of what took place than we presented in the preceding chapter.

Table 1
The New Academic Calendar

Academic Intrapreneurship

Project: **New Academic Calendar**

Scope: **Major Organization-wide Change**

Aspects: **Move from "Batch Time" toward "Real-Time"**
- Multiple Student Entry/Exit Points
- 3,7,10,14,17 Week Courses and Modules
- Continuous Registration (self-paced) Entry to Courses
- Opportunities for Innovative Curricula and Teaching Methods

Empowerment of Faculty to Support Professional Development
- Comprehensive Faculty Development Program
- Expert-Based Decision-making
- Multiple "Academic Year" Contract Options
- Opportunites for On/Off Campus Research and Study

Supporting Technologies:
- On-Line Student Registration/Records System
- On-Line Faculty Personnel System
- Faculty Development Program Decision Procedures

Project Success/Failure

Objective Measures:

Successes
- Calendar Referendum Ratified after 2 Years
- Student Enrollment Stabilized, Then Rising
- Good Enrollments in 3-Week Courses
- Some New Curricular Offerings
- Highly Successful On-Line Student Registration System
- Cessation of Tenured Faculty Layoffs
- Highly Visible Faculty Development Program: Good Participation
- Positive Internal Surveys
- Continuing Improvement of IFI, IGI Scores
- Positive External Project Audit
- Strongly Increased Extramural Grant Activity

Failures
- Low Enrollments in 7 Week Courses
- Relatively Low Rate and Slow Pace of Curricular Innovation
- Needed Better/New/Different Technologies of Communiction and Decision Making to Support a More Innovative Curriculum
- Cool Response by Accrediting Team

Perceptual Measures

Successes
- Decrease of Feeling of "UW-Zero"
- Easy Adaptation by Students to New Time Structures
- Strong, Continuing Support by UW System Administration
- Positive Response to Innovation by Visitors from Other Campuses
- Promise of Being Able to Attract Academically Stronger Students

The Innovation Project: A New Academic Calendar

In Chapter 8 we described a single, extended-search, large innovative project. This complicated set of organizational and individual forces and strategies is labeled "Academic Intrapreneurship." Thus, despite its many parts there was only one intrapreneurial effort ongoing at the University: a new Academic Calendar was proposed.

Scope: Major Organizationwide Change

The Chancellor focused on effectiveness, doing the right things. His was a strategy of hard questioning of why things were the way they were. What was the University's mission? If it served the region how could it help the atypical student (who was becoming more typical every day)? Could it accommodate the older student, the student who worked, or the part-time student? Did not a regional University in a statewide system have to understand better the nature of its funding and its survival? Were not faculty important?

In addition, the strategy embraced the use of new technology. The University was going to cross discontinuity in not one but two areas. These areas were (1) the Calendar Plan and the Technology of Time Keeping and (2) Faculty Development, which embraced Expert Decision-Making and Faculty Empowerment.

In essence, what was eventually advocated was a paradigm shift in how the academic institution was to function.

During the intrapreneurship years, analysis was present, although not in the form one might expect. There was not enough time or data (nor would it probably have been helpful) for well-thought-out, data-based, analytic deliberation of what had to be done and decision-making based on this process. Intuition and reliance on the intrapreneurs' seasoning and experience would have to suffice. And it did. This is an example of assessing what needs to be done, and then doing it! Formal planning would come later.

As noted previously, the crisis created by Oshkosh's impending "catastrophe" was an opportunity too valuable (and too painful) to pass up. Intrapreneurship permeated the Organization Decision-Making and Strategy. They were one and the same.

Throughout the period of intrapreneurship, organization decision-making and strategy incorporated elements of substantial risk. Would UW System continue to support the University through the changes? Would faculty give up valuable time to help? Would the faculty approve the changes? Had the faculty rejected the changes in either the first or second referendum, the Calendar would have reverted back to a traditional seventeen-week semester, and Faculty Development would have died. The University would have been back where it started. It would have survived but it would have lost a great opportunity.

Most Organizational Variables were positively influenced by the intrapreneurship. The organization's structure had to be redesigned to meet the intrapreneurs' goals. The organizational structure became loose and tight. The former was evident in the many committees doing important work. The efficiency (tight) side was strengthened and became functional. The organization added administrators at the top. The Vice Chancellor's office was restructured. Academic planning came into existence.

Lacking a culture and climate which accommodated intrapreneurship meant that there were no reward systems nor tradition to support such activity. At the administrative level rewards were incisive—you were either with the new Chancellor or replaced. For faculty and others who assisted in the intrapreneurship, the reward was an inner sense of satisfaction. Ideas were listened to; faculty were important. In the long run a more vital University and a Faculty Development program would be substantial rewards for organizational members.

Communication became more open. The Chancellor communicated with the faculty regularly, both personally and in more formal, written communications. The Chancellor listened to faculty. For example, by incorporating Faculty Development into the change effort, he was able to maintain faculty support and interest in the project. He was superb in reaching the opinion leaders on campus, and in working with as many of them as possible so that they would become advocates of change in their groups and the Chancellor's coalitions.

The University's control system began to serve the organization more effectively. The institution was focused on actively solving its problems, thereby forestalling UW System Administration on additional tenure layoffs and budget cutbacks. Actually, the institution was blessed with an intelligent and sensitive pair of key players who worked at System Administration. (Both of them were named Don and they were called the "Dons"; they were "our godfathers.") They were genuinely interested in a stronger UW–Oshkosh and they were supportive of *any* initiative that promised to get things moving again. The fact that the referendum passed gave them cause for pause, and they "laid off" the schedule of future budget reductions. The institution's budget was maintained and funds redirected to better serve its survival and organizational health.

Use of power within the institution was a critical organizational variable to be influenced. The new Chancellor was not only a leader but he looked for and welcomed leadership in others.

Perhaps the Chancellor's greatest strength as an intrapreneur was his ability to create action vehicles for change. The Chancellor was able to substitute positive change for the negative changes occurring at the University. By tying all of the University's functioning to the proposed Calendar and by forming a host of ad hoc committees, everything became negotiable.

In summary, the Chancellor dealt well with the complex environment. The numerous coalitions on campus were understood. He also had a good working relationship with UW System Administration. He was aided by the specter of "declining profits." The fact that there were tenure layoffs, enrollment declines, and budget payback made it easier to gain people's attention and commitment.

Aspects

The changes in the University were to be far-reaching. The University would move from Traditional Semester Time ("Batch

Time") toward "Real Time." Within the context of a new Calendar, much would be different for the entire organization.

The second major aspect of the new academic Calendar was the empowerment of faculty to support their professional development. A comprehensive Faculty Development program was initiated. Faculty would have many options for when they carried out their contractual responsibilities and when they were on their own (real professional) time.

Place of Technology

A major part of the intrapreneurial change involved technology, an important part of Academic Intrapreneurship. Technologies important to running the University were going to change. Oshkosh had to move across the discontinuity chasm from one S-curve to another. The organization had to do things differently. Doing them better might result in more efficiency and perhaps a greater student enrollment but the organization needed too much for a purely efficiency approach.

The creation of an on-line computer-based registration/record system was essential to facilitate more entry and exit points for students. Students needed to be able to register at any time. This was necessary if they were to be truly empowered in mixing their educational and noneducational (especially work) needs. The Calendar and on-line student registration represented an effort to move the organization to a "real-time" versus a "batch-time" mentality.

Other examples of newly created technologies were the development of a computerized faculty data base and the technology of expert decision-making that was used in the Faculty Development Program. We find the idea of technology in University settings to be rarely discussed and spend all of Chapter 10 on this topic.

PROJECT SUCCESS/FAILURE

The outcomes of intrapreneurship can be measured both objectively and subjectively. What did the intrapreneurs find when they looked at the product of their efforts?

Objective Successes

Objectively, the University's intrapreneurial work was a success by many criteria. For example, the Calendar referendum had been "reratified" by the faculty after two years. The intrapreneurship succeeded in being implanted in the organization because, while the innovations would continue to greatly affect the University in the years to come, the changes were oriented to the present. This allowed people to see the relevance of the changes for the immediate here and now.

The Calendar and the idea of a University of Alternatives were designed to attract students; enrollments stabilized and then rose. We cannot honestly say that the enrollment rise was directly attributable to a University of Alternatives or new Calendar per se, but the University had changed and it was perceived as being different and better.

The University began to do a much better job of defining its external environment, in understanding the organization's strengths and weaknesses, and of realizing the importance of gaining students from its own region. A concern for enrollment demanded this scanning and analysis. This example illustrates the relationship between intrapreneurship and the loop back to an institution's external environment (see Figure 2).

Many faculty revised existing courses and taught in the three-week interim classes. Not only were a sizeable number of these courses offered but enrollments in them were good. There were also other new curricular offerings, including seven-week courses beginning both at the start and middle of the fourteen-week semesters. What was possible was becoming a reality.

On-line registration and recordkeeping proved to be very effective. It allowed students to register (with good advising and direct attention to their course needs) quickly and efficiently.

Tenure layoffs were halted. As a matter of fact, recruitment of faculty to tenure-line positions continued uninterrupted.

The Faculty Development Program began and many faculty were quick to submit proposals.

People felt better about the institution and about working in it. Surveys conducted by the institution of its administration, students, and faculty yielded more positive results. A program evaluation of the University and its Calendar, conducted by a team from a major university, was also positive.

Finally, faculty efforts to obtain extramural grant monies rose dramatically.

Objective Failures

Failures, as must be the case in an intrapreneurial project as extensive as the one undertaken, are also evident. Despite the new Calendar, innovative course offerings and an innovative curriculum were slower to be adopted than had been hoped.

The attempt to empower students was not entirely successful. The student response to the scheduling opportunities that the new Calendar offered them was significantly less than anticipated.

Perceptual Successes

The process of intrapreneurship itself gave the faculty and institution greater feelings of control over their (its) own destiny, of hope, and of encouragement.

The intrapreneurial work eliminated the administrative paternalism which had been prevalent at the University. People were treated well, with integrity and respect. Most faculty felt they were a part of the institution—no longer children to be cared for by the administration. And the seeds were planted in the organization for another part of this new culture—expert power.

Funding agencies such as UW System Administration and external grant organizations liked what they saw. The "stock price" of the University would slowly rise! The intrapreneurship increased (in a monetary sense) the value of the institution.

Peer institutions both within and outside the state also liked what they heard about the changes, and representatives from other institutions came in a steady stream to learn about what had been accomplished. Inevitably they returned to their institutions impressed by what they learned.

PEOPLE, TIME FRAME, AND LUCK

Our model includes three sets of variables which span intra-preneurs' work, in all its complexity. Each must be considered in any and all phases of intrapreneurship; they are omnipresent in the intrapreneurs' world.

One set of variables involves the *personalities* of the individuals doing the intrapreneurial work. We want to know, How persistent are these people? How tolerant of ambiguity? How seasoned? How tough? These and a host of attributes contribute to intrapreneurial success or failure. As described, the Chancellor was the right person for the work which needed to get done.

A second dimension to be considered is the *time frame* of intrapreneurship and the organization. How long does it take to bring a project to fruition? We have described a project which took forty-two months to put in place, but which required many years to manage to success. One cannot assess intrapreneurial work without a clear understanding of the time frame within which it takes place. The example from our University shows the necessity and value of taking a long-term time perspective on change when assessing its value.

Third, we have deliberately included the dimension of *luck*. Successful intrapreneurship implies luck, both in choice of organizational direction and vision and in day-to-day interactions, decisions, and outcomes. An important change at the University, the core of the intrapreneurship, was to be how Time was perceived and the development of technologies to manage it. But this innovative and important conceptualization was not a brilliant insight into how to save Oshkosh, nor did it stem from extended discussion of a planning group or a dominant coalition. It was completely fortuitous. Had the Chancellor had different interests and worked with different people at the University, the foci and nature of intrapreneurship at the campus would also have been different. What looks like so perfect a solution was one idea out of many which could have been chosen.

The intrapreneurship succeeded because it was to offer a win–win scenario to UW System administration, to most faculty, and to students. The Chancellor wanted to find some way of restoring pride in the campus and in what people were doing. In the absence of fiscal resources to work with, an alternative was to redesign and create distinctiveness. The Calendar and everything that went with it was a vehicle for that purpose. The intrapreneurship used the materials on-site, existing programs, people, and ideas.

Intrapreneurs do not worry about that which they cannot control. They also must give up control to serendipity and the fates. Important events are often not planned; important people come and go. For example, the chief sponsor in the organization may leave. Or the economy may change, making the intrapreneurial product less feasible. Technology can surprise an intrapreneurial team. Another organization may reach the market first. In the case of our University, the chief executive officer worked very hard to develop support and relationships with UW System. But there was no guarantee that he would receive support from System in the form of no additional tenure layoffs and no additional budget payback. The element of "dumb luck" cannot be ignored.

THE FUTURE

The intrapreneurship left the University better able to adapt to, predict, and embrace the future with some confidence. Chapter 15 (Epilogue) provides a discussion of what transpired after the intrapreneurial Chancellor left and how the University has fared in the subsequent decade. An examination of the long-term effects of intrapreneurial work should always be undertaken.

Chapter 10
Technology and the Intrapreneur

Intrapreneurial activity is high-energy stuff, full of excitement, heat, and emotion. Technology and systems, such as information systems, both paper-driven and computer-based, are usually thought of as rational and cool, the stuff of engineers and technocrats. Too often technology and systems are dismissed as something that will bend to the new vision, as if they can easily respond to the heat and passion of the collective will. They cannot and do not do so easily.

Intrapreneurship places demands on the organization's underlying systems and technologies. Yet many intrapreneurs seldom understand, and still less often appreciate, the role of technology in both supporting and permitting the development of a "new way of doing things" within an organization. Intrapreneurs who have gained the organization's permission to "try" their ideas must be aware that there is a rather large "second shoe" yet to be dropped. Vision and communication of good ideas will move ahead of the changes in supporting technology which are required for the vision to become a reality. Even in our experience, in which the "techies" began work (before even formally requested to do so) on computer technology to support the intrapreneurial changes, they were behind schedule in what was needed. As slow as technological change is, one can expect that people will change more rapidly than the technologies which exist to support their work within the organization.

Remember our earlier definition of technology. Broadly conceived, technology is the application of systematic approaches to the management or understanding of any part or process in an organization. As noted in Chapter 6, that which is technical (the scientific and mechanical) is only one part of technology. Many, many different technologies are involved in the management of a university, such as budgeting, cost control, purchasing, time management, resource allocation, curricula, and so on.

The intrapreneurship we have described included two key notions that would place enormous demands on the technologies available within the institution to support them. The first idea was the fundamental restructuring of the "macro" dimension of Time. This included the scheduling of classes, student enrollment periods, and faculty work periods. We refer to this macro definition of Time by beginning the word with a capital letter.

The second idea was that *faculty* should work in an institution in which they were responsible for the allocation of dollars to support their professional development. This would be accomplished within a culture of expert decision-making.

In this chapter we discuss these two examples of technology—expert decision-making and Timekeeping. Before we do this, however, the reader needs to understand the state of technology at the University before the intrapreneurship.

THE UNIVERSITY'S TECHNOLOGIES BEFORE INTRAPRENEURSHIP

The information systems, both electronic and paper-driven, at UW–Oshkosh in 1974 were typical of that period. The basic operational systems (Markus, 1984), which structure the work tasks of the organization and rationalize and routinize work, for example, registration, billing, fee collection, financial aids, and grade reporting, were functional, although structured as batch processes. For example, registration was conducted in a gymnasium, with faculty and staff on the periphery handing out computer cards representing individual class seats, while students scrambled from point to point to make up a workable and productive class schedule. At predetermined times, a gate-keeper would allow more students into the arena to participate in this complicated space-and-time puzzle game.

Monitoring and control systems, which track and support evaluation of individual or group performance toward goal performance, were rudimentary and were supportive of centralized, legitimate authority. (In other organizations, monitoring and control systems are able to support decentralization of authority.) The organization had expanded virtually out of control in the late 1960s; consequently mature control systems had not developed. The control systems that did exist focused on control of functions such as student registration and billing. Computer technology was just moving into the educational organization for administrative purposes.

The planning and decision systems, which supported the intellectual functions of choice within the organization, were manual and paper-driven. They supported a highly centralized, strongly batch-driven process. Since everything major in the University such as budget, registration, tabulating enrollments, and so on, took place at only certain times of the year, this made sense.

Communication systems, which play a critical role in educating and informing organizational members of problems and opportunities on the horizon, were even less developed.

Interorganizational systems, such as formal linkages between the University and the UW System office, were virtually nil. While the recently merged University of Wisconsin System was laying in some new interorganizational systems to strengthen its monitoring and control function, common data definitions that serve as the cornerstone for such efforts had not yet been achieved. Thus the formal system links were relatively immature (and radically different than today), a fact that permitted the Calendar innovation to develop more rapidly than might otherwise have been the case.

The information systems that did exist strongly reflected the basic time cycles of the organization and its mission—teaching. They were synchronized to two major academic cycles, Fall and

Spring, and the annual budget process. A close examination of the information system technologies revealed the following to the intrapreneurs:

- Time was treated in a batch fashion, not as real Time.
- The organization valued formal bureaucracy and a strong top-down management style.
- Decision-making was relegated to those with legitimate power.
- The technologies were not designed to respond to opportunity. They supported a formal and slow-moving distribution of the University's assets such as space, finances, and personnel.

These operational systems would need to support new products if the intrapreneurs were to succeed. The intrapreneurs recognized the link between authority and power within the organization and, therefore, all of the information systems were of obvious interest to them.

DECENTRALIZED DECISION-MAKING AS TECHNOLOGY

Information systems and information technology are *not* all computer-driven but include *all* of the processes that relate to the movement of information and implementation of decisions within the organization. This includes the framing and scheduling of decisions, the articulation of choices and alternatives, and the fast, reliable implementation of decisions. It was these functions, and in particular the decision-making one, that needed to succeed in new ways if a new intrapreneurial support structure was to be successfully implanted.

The University decision-making issue related to *who* would make the resource allocations to individual faculty and *how*. Once the who was determined to be the Faculty Development Board, the new technology of expert decision-making could be shaped and put in place. This new technology (with a strong link and relationship to the Board's culture) obviously was successful.

The Board's decision technology had to be efficient, one that respected the commodity that is so important to an expert—

Time. Experts need efficiency. While they view the world with a timeless perspective, they know that there simply is not enough time to pursue all the good ideas that they will encounter.

Finally, the decision technology had to be effective; one where problems and issues did not persist unendingly. In meetings and decision-making, Board members did not induce legal or procedural arguments; these belong in the world of the political or legitimate cultures. They focused on the really important decisions and on effectiveness questions.

Meetings were regularly scheduled several months in advance, and occurred at frequent intervals. Agendas, always written and sent out prior to the meeting (with attachments to permit study prior to the assembly of the experts), were built around specific proposals or proposed draft policy changes. Unstructured discussions were rare. Special meetings for these purposes were scheduled two times per year.

Within the Board meetings, a strong consensus model prevailed. Decisions on proposals or policy with close votes did not stick; they were not real. Close votes indicated that the Board members were not using the same criteria to assess a proposal, or did not share the same expert values when discussing new or different policies. If the Board could not endorse an expert's judgment in a near-complete consensus, it would listen some more. The Board chair always sought permission to take a particular direction to seek resolution for a thorny issue and brought back a recommendation for endorsement prior to "deciding."

The Board sought the opinion of the "most expert" within its ranks on each issue, but the decision-making technology did not allow "cheap shots" nor "quick hits." In a group setting "quick hits" take place when someone knows more than others and the group moves to a decision because this person knows the best or right answer, *without the group being educated on the issue*. "Quick hits" reflect an intellectual disdain for others. The decision-making was designed to support an expert culture in which there was respect for others. Those who knew took the time to educate others so they also could know and understand. Then a vote took place.

A special attempt was made to reflect priorities in building the agendas. Important matters were always considered first. This is similar to the approach used for individual time-management programs. Once the meeting was over, almost always on time, the paperwork moved quickly. Recommendations from the Board went to the Vice Chancellor within the day, and he acted quickly, a feat not possible in a more political organization.

The importance of timely and good decision-making is that it differentiates the expert culture from that of the legitimate/ political ones, and reinforces the expert's participation in the process. All outcomes were immediately posted in the University's internal communication organ.

TIMEKEEPING AS TECHNOLOGY

Timekeeping and its management can be conceptualized as technology. As such it will affect other technologies, such as information systems, operating in an organization. The concept of "batched" versus "real" Time is an important one and merits example and discussion.

The traditional university calendar is a special example of how Time cycles shape both the exercise of individual priorities and the supporting information systems within the organization. Students seek access to their classes and organization's instructional assets. They are permitted primary exercise of choice typically two times each year. (Summer school is a third choice time, although used less frequently.) These choice situations are "batched" early in the fall and in the spring.

In other areas as well, universities save up tasks for weeks or months at a time and do them all at once. Student enrollment is counted each semester, all at once. Faculty all begin a contractual year at the same time, all at once. These are examples of "batched" Time.

In this manner, the traditional university does not run in "real Time." In contrast, can you imagine an airline that scheduled flights only during the first weeks of September and February? Real Time implies taking care of tasks as they arise. One can make an airline reservation, within reason, anytime one wants.

The same is true for placement of orders to buy or sell stocks on the New York Stock Exchange. Our society is moving to a real-Time mode, as evidenced in twenty-four hour grocery stores, cable television shop-at-home channels, and a host of other real-Time technologies.

The concept of real and batch Time also has important applications for faculty. The collegial ideal of the university insists that the individual faculty member participate in the collective decision-making of the organization. This suggests a distribution of authority and power within a time frame that is *not* batch-driven since the "real world" is increasingly "real Time." Budget issues must be decided when governors or legislatures act. Conferences and professional opportunities come and go, without respect for the teaching calendar. Implementation of the collegial ideal requires the distribution of authority in its control and decision systems. Moreover, it implies creating an academic organization which operates on real and not batch Time as much as possible.

In academia, theoretically, if faculty want to read a journal article or book, think about an idea, or attend to their research or writing, they can do this whenever they have free time. But at universities such as ours, the reality is that free time is in short supply and is not always available when needed or wanted.

In most regional universities, faculty also seek access to assets to further their professional development. For most, teaching is a source of enjoyment. But it is not something one needs to seek out; it is automatically assigned. What must be individually sought is access to professional development resources, that is, travel dollars, research assistants, supply monies, federal or private grant funds, and, perhaps most important, personal professional Time. In a university with a large teaching load, the semester Time cycle of the students and the teaching workload carry the professional activity of the faculty in their wake. A faculty member must "batch" good ideas and work on them (research, writing, etc.) only when not teaching.

While, ideally, professional work should be continuous, it is not. It reflects a batch-Time process. And because of this, the quality of the faculty's professional work suffers. Thus faculty experience, and must manage, a conflict inherent in their professional lives. The nature of professional development Time is that it *is* (or should be) continuous. The nature of teaching is that it must be scheduled, since it involves the intersection of two or more people. The conflict of continuous Time for professional development with teaching classes (batch Time) is what is at the heart of many universities' problems. Ideally, a passion for ideas knows no artificial barriers of Time.

Time management teaches us to not let *urgent* needs replace *vital* ones. Yet this is precisely what the traditional calendar in academia does. The vital needs of faculty to grow, to write, to do research, and to live in the world of ideas conflict with the urgent needs (at least at an institution such as ours) to teach.

The Restructuring of Time

Students had choices, but they were confined to making them within the mad scramble of a bullpen registration only two times per year. Faculty made few real choices related to their professional development. Authority to approve the expenditure of funds or the reallocation of Time within a faculty contract for professional development was tightly centralized. It was a simple world indeed. But it was not working.

Into this simple structure came the notion of completely restructuring Time for both students and faculty. A Time-management system, new to the institution, was to be introduced. The proposed modular Calendar was a dramatic new approach to giving faculty and students new and much more varied choices in their collective arenas of professional development. It assumed that Time was a valuable professional resource to be allocated. It further assumed that students and faculty would exercise those choices much more frequently and freely than they had previously. It assumed that a student enrolling in a class, or a faculty member pursuing a research idea, should be a *real Time* rather than batch process. This concept was the keystone to the innovation.

The decision to proceed with real Time forced the intrapreneurs to go "back to the basics" with respect to their information systems and technologies. There were many operations to support, and monitoring and controlling them in this new real

Time environment was much more demanding. The new technologies would have to support people in ways they never had and much more often—daily! As a result, there were many more decisions to be made. And there was to be a great deal of change, requiring much more effective communication systems than were in place.

In our model, Time for both teaching and faculty development was to be as continuous as the intrapreneurs could make it. The Calendar broke Time into smaller lumps, as close as the intrapreneurs could get Time to a real-Time process. If both teaching and professional development could incorporate a real-time technology, more innovative use of time and a higher quality of the work done in both areas might result. And a major problem for the faculty might be resolved.

The Class Schedule

Not surprisingly, the initial focus of supporting technology was on the key product of the organization: the class schedule—the intersection of courses, students, faculty, and classroom facilities. The old class schedule was replaced by a seemingly bewildering complicated array of choices of seven-, ten-, fourteen-, and seventeen-week courses. Students had to learn to read a much more complicated paper-driven class schedule, and make choices to build much more complicated course schedules. The choices were so many and so complicated that they could not be placed in a matrix in a meaningful way on a computer screen or printout, which are constrained to two-dimensional matrices or representations. As a consequence, class schedules were printed by cutting and pasting various alternatives (department, course numbers, when offered, etc.) so that they made some sense. Students could choose from fourteen-week classes, seven-week classes (some starting at the beginning and some at the middle of a semester), three-week classes, and so on. Could they do it? No one knew for sure.

Simple patterns, therefore, become complex. For example:

• How does one present a real–Time class schedule that does not read like an airline schedule? The answer is that one cannot. Had the vast array of alternative times for courses continued, the course schedule book would have been as complicated and difficult to read as an airline schedule.

- How can "academic progress" be defined when students start and stop willy-nilly? The answer was to count the number of credits a student had registered for regardless of when these credits were earned.

- How can the University run food service and residence halls on a real–Time basis? At our University a typical dormitory contract entails the length of a semester. The system proved flexible enough to accommodate students anytime they were taking courses on campus. The University operates like a hotel.

It was not an easy nine months to develop the answers to these and *many* other questions of technology.

The University needed a lot of new information systems, both paper-driven and computer-based, and in a hurry. The intrapreneurs had to find ways to report grades, to keep track of student records, to count the number of students enrolled in the University, and to establish student credit hours.

The intrapreneurs encountered a situation in which the people who oversaw the administrative processes had no clear idea of what they were trying to accomplish within the context of the innovation, and even less of a notion of how to do it! Good systems designs require a clear vision of what is to be accomplished. They also require a "bottom-up" approach, with a clear definition of needs. This is particularly true for operational systems. However, the normal systems design and development process would not work in this University's environment. Systems had to be conceptualized by teams of individuals with little first-hand experience in the operational areas to be affected. What the intrapreneurs asked is that new systems be simply tested in the ideal and jammed into place. It was rough on people.

Professional Development Timekeeping

The new Faculty Development Program presented faculty with a multiplicity of choices. Within any contiguous two-year period, faculty could arrange a teaching and professional development schedule. Faculty could decide when they wanted to teach, within the limits of eight Calendar modules and the needs of their department. Any time not spent teaching could be spent in professional development activities funded by the new Faculty Development Board.

Operational problems were almost immediately identified (and mastered) in the mundane area of payroll, where policies and procedures had to be bent to "connect" the realities of the new Calendar to the inflexibilities of the state's faculty payroll system. It is the seemingly simple and mundane control systems which can stifle the most effective and creative intrapreneurial idea. The great challenge was to find a way to pay faculty for professional development activities at *any time* during the year in ways which met state approval. Had a way not been found the idea of real (faculty development) Time could have died.

More serious monitoring and control problems soon emerged with the realization that not all faculty would start and complete their contractual obligations within the traditional semester-based rhythms of the historical organization. For example:

- What would faculty *do* during the Calendar time modules within which they were contracted but not scheduled to teach a class? Most faculty behaved professionally, attending to their own professional work and attempting to be as collegial as possible in meeting department and University needs.
- How would faculty committees function if members moved on and off at each of the eight modular start-stop dates in the new organizational Time structures? Most faculty maintain committee work even when they are not teaching.

Not surprisingly, the monitoring and control issue was of highest concern to the "managers" of the organization. They moved rather quickly to develop a paper-based technology to maintain a record, with appropriate signatures for accountability, of who was doing what, when, and where.

But the other side of the coin was to be the more interesting to the intrapreneurs. How would they structure information systems that effectively *communicated* the decision options that were now available to faculty to promote their individual and collective professional development? What sort of *planning and decision support* systems would be needed?

The strategic problem was one of supporting decision-making in a totally new arena, the restructuring of a professional's time obligation to the organization. The problem was further complicated by the need to decentralize some of the decision-making into a group (the Faculty Development Board) that was not experienced in making such decisions.

First, the intrapreneurs had to develop communication patterns that would effectively provide each faculty with the full range of choices available to them within the new Calendar's flexibility. In other words the "high technology" had to be complemented by what Naisbitt (1984) calls "high touch." Then technologies which would quickly transport individual plans and decisions into the resource distribution channels for action had to be established. Given this context, it is not surprising that a new stress point developed within a short time in the area of Faculty Personnel systems. The paper-driven technology of the past had been adequate for the long time cycles associated with the old calendar. The shorter cycles of the new Calendar required a more responsive information technology.

Here again, the intrapreneurs encountered the stark reality that those who best knew how the organization's faculty personnel functions were managed did not share in the vision of the Calendar's potential for its faculty personnel. The projected managers of the system were not capable of participating in its design. As in other areas, the information systems to support this function were conceived, designed, and developed by intrapreneurs outside of the faculty personnel management area. As the new systems were installed, the staff manning the faculty personnel management function in the organization moved on.

FOUR LESSONS ON THE RELATIONSHIP OF TECHNOLOGY WITH INTRAPRENEURSHIP

One can anticipate that any move to strengthen the intrapreneurial environment will require the redistribution of choice, decision-making, and the authority to act. Changes in who has power in an organization influence its technological support systems. For example, one typically finds that intrapreneurial work drives new demands for information. As a result, enhanced monitoring and control systems will be needed for the "less tightly held" organization. Stronger communication systems are needed to make more individuals more fully aware of the new options available to them. Planning and decision systems need to be available to more individuals. The looseness of a more intrapreneurial organization demands tight efficiency from its technology if organizational members are to benefit from their new ventures, autonomy, and/or empowerment.

Second, the intrapreneurs must realistically anticipate the need to design the new systems "the wrong way," that is, from the top down. This is why intrapreneurs need sponsors and support from influential others in an organization. Sometimes intrapreneurs need the power to demand that certain technology changes take place. Sometimes they need the ability to transfer people from one function or unit to another. Intrapreneurs' visions will not be shared (accepted) by all of those who are exercising decision-making in the more tightly held organization. This is why visions must be grounded in reality. Vision by itself is seldom influential to convince others to give up power and decision-making, that is, commit themselves to an alternative reality. But functional, rational arguments supported by data can be persuasive. Those with legitimate and political power can be expected to oppose intrapreneurial work, or at least to have their own agendas for outcome and redistribution of power. Even those who are rationally sympathetic to the need to distribute authority need a functioning model to participate in the design process, not a model of vision and "pie in the sky" future vitality. And some will simply disagree with the whole notion, and work to subvert the effort.

Third, people are important in the technology of intrapreneurship. The prominence of computer-based information systems in organizations depends on the mission, purpose, and products of the organization. "High tech" information systems are typically *not* prominent in the administration of teaching organizations and they were not in our University. In this domain of the intellect, teaching, an intensely human enterprise, is the prominent function. It claims top priority in the competition for scarce resources. In academia one does not have to wait for the "right" technical support to engage in intrapreneurship. Especially in academia, the technology is one of people: leading them, cajoling them, and using their talents. Some whose expertise is needed will be lazy or resist because the design of new technologies is hard work! The nature of the intrapreneurship being considered will suggest the type and location of the new technologies that will be needed. Key individuals who share the vision, and who also understand the requirements of the function to be supported by the new technology, need to be identified and positioned to "make it happen" in the systems development arena. These are not computer problems, they are real problems which involve people.

Last, one must anticipate a great many "people problems" as the new technologies to support intrapreneurial activity are implemented within the organization. The redistribution and dispersion of authority to access and use organizational resources will not come easily. Those who "have" will use every means to hold. They will use every possible barrier to prevent the movement of authority away from themselves.

The intrapreneurship at our organization required a higher level of information technology than was available to support planning, decision-making, and to generally "keep the organization whole." Development of needed technologies did not come easily. Without skilled leadership in the technical arena to effectively deal with these issues, the intrapreneurship would have failed. To paraphrase from Ashby (1966), an intrapreneur who cannot weave his technology into the fabric of the organization cannot claim even to be a good technologist.

Chapter 11
Intrapreneurship and Its Effect on Culture

Sometimes one of the products and processes which emanate from intrapreneurs' work is a new culture in the organization. In our case this was to be the expert power of a new group on campus, the Faculty Development Board. Had the organization and/or the intrapreneurship been different, we would be writing about other cultures than expert power and other groups on campus—curricular, political (Faculty Senate), computer, admissions, and so on. While we write about a development of an expert culture, it is important to note that this is only one of an unlimited number of cultures which intrapreneurship can spawn. We focus on why and how one creates a new culture.

THE CULTURE AT UW–O BEFORE INTRAPRENEURSHIP

The culture at UW–O in the 1960s was one of valuing the status quo of stability. People were nice to each other. It was a paternalistic time with the administration taking care of the faculty. Being a typical regional university was vision enough for the future if anyone had vision at all. Communications were closed. This was not a culture of meritocracy.

Largely as a product of growth and stress, the culture of UW–O in 1974 was split into three portions: (1) the "old culture" that was based on notions of legitimate power, that is, a person's ability to influence because of position, such as President or Dean, was still strong in many quarters but had become weaker because of the failure of the organization (e.g., recent enrollment decline and tenure layoffs); (2) a counterculture based on values related to political power, centered on the Faculty Senate and the various professional unions; and (3) an informal culture (the Druid one) based on the idealistic values of the traditional university, carried by the group of "new Ph.D.s" who had been recruited under the dream of doctoral programs at UW–O.

The historical organization at Oshkosh was strong on legitimate power; administrators made decisions, not faculty. Administrators were often patronizing and some faculty (the "pols"), who simply sought the same type of power, elected to pursue this by establishing a political culture. In frustration, some genuinely expert faculty had aligned themselves with the "pols," not realizing that in doing so they had turned their backs on the expert culture that is the tradition of true Druid (university) communities.

The Need for a New Culture

Universities evolving out of a legitimate power structure (such as former teacher colleges that try to grow up) are similar to the development of business organizations. In both types of organizations management typically has no tradition of respecting the expert structures, and as these organizations expand they grow into red tape bureaucracies. This is particularly true of most public universities, because their tradition is a culture of legitimate power. (Private academic institutions may have a stronger culture in their pasts, either expert or religious, which helps maintain identity and vitality during periods of growth and change.) Managers in bureaucratic academic organizations use the red tape mechanisms to gain access to, and hoard, resources. And as resources become scarcer, the technology of red tape becomes ever more powerful and efficient.

Innovations, especially those that cross the boundaries of the "hoarding units," need red tape cutters to get at dollars, variances of policy, new procedures, and, most important, people and talent. This is the world of experts, people who *know* things and *can do* things. Intrapreneurship becomes the catalyst for the basic conflict between expert, political, and legitimate powers.

If an organization is to value intrapreneurship and new ventures, the need is to "inculcate" the organization with a new set of values. These values will become visible in new rituals and may, over time, serve to support a change in the organization's basic assumptions about its world. These new values, in our case expert decision-making and an expert culture, compete with the internal environment which may already be in delicate tension. In our case the internal environment was marked by tension between two subcultures, one based on legitimate and the other on political power.

In summary, several needs existed in the University for a culture of experts. One was the need to make a recalcitrant bureaucracy more responsive to and congruent with institutional needs. A second was to accommodate growth and new values. A third was to support the intrapreneurial process. But there is another reason to strive for a culture of experts in academe. Faculty and their disciplines thrive, and universities are the most vital, when expert power is evident. In their purest forms, universities value expert opinion.

The problem at UW–O was that legitimate and political power were not serving the University well. The situation required a different type of decision-making process for the University, a reversal wherein decision-making would move from a process of top (administration)–down to the bottom (faculty)–up. As the intrapreneurship progressed, experts (faculty, academic staff) had to be brought into the decision-making arena with administrators. What evolved formed the basis for a rational, expert decision-making system, not a political one. The vision of a "true university," as one in which experts prevail, followed from, but did not lead, the process of relegating political and legitimate power to lesser roles.

A new culture was possible because of a "technological seduction" (Schein, 1985b). The introduction of new technologies as discussed in Chapter 10—Time and Expert Decision-Making—coupled with a new Calendar, continuous registration, and

Faculty Development, allowed and perhaps forced a change in culture. But the intrapreneurial changes were not simply to be "plopped" into the University to fit in, or not fit in, with the already existing cultures. If the changes were to take root, a new culture had to take root as well. While the intrapreneurshp took place over a relatively brief time, (forty-two months), establishing a new culture mandated a long-term view of time, measured in years and years.

A CULTURE OF EXPERT DECISION-MAKING

The underlying value of an expert culture is the quality and correctness of ideas. Those individuals with quality ideas, especially if the area of demonstrated expertise is in demand and demonstrated by few others, will possess more expert power. The expert culture flourishes high on the hierarchy of human needs, especially in an academic setting. Political and legitimate cultures address lower level survival needs. At the time of the intrapreneurship at UW–O, the environment was one of survival, that is, scarce resources and visible threats to security. There was little budget to spare, and tenure layoff was a reality. To plant and "grow" an expert culture, and appeal to the higher needs of faculty, would take special skill. But there was no choice if the organization was to move forward. An expert culture would have to be protected from its environment, encapsulated in a fashion that permitted the pure form of the organism to gain experience and become established.

INCEPTION AND SCOPING OF THE DEVELOPMENT PROGRAM

There were two major problems in instituting a new culture at our University, problems inherent in forming any new culture. The first was to design the cultural system. There was nowhere to go for guidance. How to define and describe the new culture, and its reason for being, had to be clearly thought through and communicated to organizational members. Part of this problem was how to design procedures that would permit the Faculty Development Program (the symbol of an expert culture) to function as an expert decision body when this was completely foreign to its parent organization.

The second problem was implementation of the new culture. What was needed was an environment with a low administrative but high faculty profile. The latter was a thorny problem. How does one gain the participation of experts (faculty) who place a supreme value on their professional time?

The group that met the first problem was the Faculty Development Program Committee, which during the intrapreneurial years worked under the Chancellor. Its membership was selected by the Chancellor and represented faculty who had not been drawn into the power struggle between the legitimate and political subcultures. They exemplified the importance of people in organizational efforts. The time to take a reflective intensive view of an intrapreneurial effort is before one selects the intrapreneurial team. The time lines under which they were to work were incredibly tight. They had an impossible schedule to meet: only eight weeks to conceive and define a whole new program in uncharted terrain. It was this urgency which kept the problem-solving and design effort on track. The group *had* to get the job done; the task was both *vital* and *urgent*.

The choice of faculty for the Faculty Development Program Committee was critical to what would follow. As individuals, and collectively, they shared the following:

1. An Optimistic World View: Although the situation was grim in the overall organization, these were optimists who believed in the University's future as a professional, expert organization.

2. A Long-Term View: These were individuals who could see along very long time lines.

3. A Clear Vision: These individuals knew what an expert culture looked like. They valued professional development rather than political action. Their purpose was clear.

4. A Well-Defined Scope: The Calendar Papers had given them a clearly defined problem.

5. An Important Agenda: They felt the importance of the task in which they were involved. They would give time to the future of the organization even though this work competed with the demands of remaining vital in their professions.

CREATING A NEW CULTURE

The mechanism by which a new culture of experts was to be introduced into the organization was the fledgling Faculty Development Board. This arena had to be designed to nurture individual faculty and their collective development. This direction was consistent with the most basic premise of the innovation—faculty had to exert a greater degree of control over their professional lives. Collectively, for better or for worse, faculty had to be in control of Faculty Development.

The Need for Leadership

The senior administrator who chaired the Board during its early years knew what would be required to establish a culture of expert power within the group. He worked hard on issues of trust and open communication (Deal and Kennedy, 1982) and at developing the skills of the faculty members of the Board. His was a long-term time perspective. If an expert culture was to survive, he had to get the faculty to "own" this culture. The culture could not be created merely by his words; it would have to become the shared history of Board members (Schein, 1985b). He would succeed because the culture he was building reflected "intrinsically appealing beliefs and values" (Sathe, 1985) of the faculty. The Board is a good example of the percept that any group which meets regularly may develop common understandings (culture) distinct from those of other groups in the organization (Louis, 1985).

The Development Board leader also succeeded because of what he paid attention to: his reactions to critical incidents (attacks on the program, tightness of funds, etc.); his role modeling, teaching, and coaching; and his criteria for recruitment of new Board members. (Schein, 1985a, calls these "embedding mechanisms.") His advice, decisions, and rationale were consistent with an expert culture. He tried to get the Board members, who represented many different disciplines, to look at the "whole picture." He kept the Board on task, diminishing its needs for talk or conversation for the sake of debate. He taught by what he said and by sharing how he arrived at the opinions he did. And he talked in a plain, uncomplicated, direct way.

The focus was always on the issue at hand or the precedents the Board had set and/or future implications of a decision. He did not blame faculty when they attacked the Board or wrote angry memos to it. He helped the Board learn to understand how academicians think and feel when required to write proposals to fund their work, thereby putting their skills and expertise on the line in public. He helped the Board explore parts of the University with which they had little experience in order to expand their problem-solving abilities and understand the dynamics of the University. He expected faculty on the Board to work hard. By expecting faculty commitment to the Board he helped establish it. He took the role of experts and the Board's responsibilities seriously. There was a passion which emanated from him for this work.

The Importance of Letting a New Culture Grow

The power conflict between the legitimate and political subcultures in the University was avoided. Both left the established decision technology alone. Academic business without politics! Two key events occurred to make this possible. When the Calendar Papers were being ratified, the Faculty Senate debated them very briefly. In ratifying them the Senate disenfranchised themselves. The political culture voted to sanction something which affected each of its members greatly but which it would not control. In other words, it decided it would have no formal influence on Faculty Development matters. And the Faculty Senate "pols" to this day have never seriously "come at" the Development Program.

The second key event involves the Vice Chancellor and others with legitimate power. When the Calendar Papers were approved, the documents' language clearly allowed the Vice Chancellor to be a voting member of the Faculty Development Board. Yet the first Vice Chancellor never did this. His absence was beneficial; it allowed the faculty members more ownership of the program. The two subsequent Vice Chancellors have never personally attended meetings either. Perhaps the first Vice

Chancellor was told by the Chancellor to leave Faculty Development alone—possible but improbable. A more probable explanation is that the Vice Chancellor was so identified with the University planning process that he did not want to get involved with Faculty Development. It is also possible that the Vice Chancellor felt no passion for Faculty Development and, to be sure, passion was required.

This freedom from both legitimate and political cultures set the tone for an expert culture. The originality of the idea and the quality of the pursuit are the proper issues of an expert community that is a university. And on the Faculty Development Board these are the *sole* determinants of which ideas are to be pursued!

The Importance of Design

Design must symbolize and reflect a culture if it is to succeed. A low administrative and bureaucratic profile was adopted to keep a focus and visibility on decisions and outcomes. This was different from the hoarding units' strategies and processes and kept the program safe from faculty attack. Rules would be clear and directly related to the program; paperwork would also be kept to a minimum.

The responsiblity for "managing" the program was given to a senior administrator who had a lot of other things to do. The identity of the program could be developed as one of "Faculty Development"; the program did not belong to an administrator. A separate budget line was avoided for the administrative part of the program.

Faculty Development resources would go to the faculty, not to managing the program. This forced a very efficient operation with low administrative overhead. The administrative part of the program would defer to the program's true purpose, faculty development. This is fitting for an expert culture.

The Board's internal environment focused on people's ideas and professional practices, not people's positions within the organization. It was an apolitical approach. If there were to be symbols of the program they would relate to expert decision-making and the professional development of faculty, not to administrative trappings.

Some such symbols were developed. For example, a public image was formed of a program linked to strong, respected groups external to the University such as the Lilly Endowment. The Lilly Foundation provided funds for the program early in its life and also provided funds for its evaluation after several years.

The Importance of How Problems Are Solved

A decision-making technology (See Chapter 10) consistent with a culture of experts was adopted. This approach to problem solving respected the expert community. The focus was on serving faculty. Any idea for a faculty's professional development could be discussed or submitted in a formal proposal. In its frequent written communications; formal meetings, all open to the faculty; and individual contact with faculty the message communicated was one of respect, helpfulness, and collegiality.

To make best use of the decision-making technology the style of the meetings was open, honest and, collegial. Since expert decision-making was valued, Board members were urged to speak their minds. The focus was always on ideas. To focus on personalities was to violate the cultural norms, values, and beliefs. As a result, the group had a great deal of affection for each other. They stood together in their decisions, even if they, as individuals, did not always agree with some of the resolutions they reached. Again, these are assumptions and values of the "long haul."

The Need for Trust and Integrity

The Board members came to trust each other. Moreover, their assumption about faculty members who submitted proposals was "Theory Y," a belief that faculty members would successfully complete their projects. Trust and integrity permeated all areas of the expert culture.

The Importance of Money

The bureaucracy-forming pressures of a tight budget were avoided by having ample funds ($200,000) to initiate the program, thereby effectively defusing budget as a potential issue. Providing this amount of start-up capability was a difficult decision for the University and was done within an overall environment in which competition for dollars to hire teachers was high. The Chancellor had promised to use some dollars taken from decreased faculty pay for summer school to support the Faculty Development Program and he did so. These funds were quickly supplemented by extramural dollars. For example, a $7500 award from the National Association of College and University Business Officers was given to the Faculty Development Program by the Chancellor. Since 1974 the original corpus has been adjusted for faculty raises each year. All these budget-related matters permitted the fledgling culture to focus on the value of experts, quality of ideas, and expression.

Competition for early Faculty Development dollars was high. But expert decision-making implies that good ideas which are well stated and strongly presented will be funded. And they were. A high level of quality was set and maintained. Money was not the issue. Culture was. There were low-quality proposals which were denied funding. Rather than use up budget (a hoarding mentality) for its own sake the emphasis was on supporting good faculty projects. When the budget was not expended it was returned to the University control system. This assisted the program in being perceived as a team player. It also meant that if there were years when monies were in short supply a request for additional funds had strong weight. The Board displayed integrity in handling its budget.

The Need for Codification and Continuity

As the fledgling culture gained experience, it codified its procedures and values into a Faculty Development Handbook which was distributed to all faculty, management, and academic staff members of the organization. It served as a visible symbol of the changeless nature of the program's purpose and values.

The program would outlast those with the original vision. A testament was written. It codified the new decision technologies and the new rules.

To make it harder to be destroyed by its political and legitimate environments, the design made it difficult for major procedural or policy changes to be effected. This allowed the culture to grow and develop, while at the same time it prevented the technology of decision-making from being perverted. The intent was to insulate the new program from early capriciousness. The focus was to be on a singular vision of Faculty Development and an expert culture.

To ensure the continuation of its internal culture, three-year rotating terms for Board members were established. This allowed continuity to be built into the structure and ensured that there would be "sages of the past" on the Board. Some members even served more than one term, thereby strengthening even more continuity and expert culture. "[T]he strength, clarity, and degree of integration of a corporate culture or subculture is directly proportional to the stability of the membership of the group, the length of time the group has been together, and the intensity of the collective learning that has taken place" (Schein, 1985b, p. 26). All this also served to reinforce the changeless, timeless characteristic of the culture.

The Need for Predictability

The decision-making outputs of the group had to be, and did become, predictable. Faculty knew the basis for decisions to fund, or not fund, a proposal. This was important to the success of the venture, since it was an arena to which independent entrepreneurs would turn for resources to pursue their dreams. And dreams do not come and go—indeed the really good ones outlast a lifetime.

The Need for Authority

Another very important outcome was creating the perception of authority. Many faculty came to assume that a recommendation from the Board was a decision of the organization. This reinforced the value of expert power as something to be acquired so that it could be exercised. The decision-making technology was also effective in that decisions made by the expert group were *very rarely* reversed by those with legitimate power. On this latter point, the perception of authority was made stronger by several unsuccessful challenges against the Board's integrity and resources. The Deans periodically made "a run at" the Board's budget, but failed. The "pols" spread rumors and innuendo about the Board's misuse of funds, favoritism, being influenced by administrators, and so on, but the Board's integrity prevailed. And, on a more subtle level, as mentioned earlier, the three Vice Chancellors to whom the Board has reported all have chosen *not* to participate as peers on the Board, even though the chartering documents included this provision. Their lack of direct participation contributes to the independent expert authority of the Faculty Development Board.

The Importance of Responsibility

Periods of group reinforcement were frequent. The Board took on some tough issues. How do intrapreneurs convince outsiders, and especially the more rational faculty inside the organization, that the changes are worthwhile? They evaluate. The Board instituted evaluation of its own functioning. It showed responsibility. This occurred in the second year of its life. For this, a full-time staff member, external to the University, was hired with extramural monies. He interviewed every faculty member and administrator on campus! This satisfied the need for data. The evaluation work also provided control information which was useful in the program's administration.

The idea of evaluation became part of the Board's culture. In the past decade, the University has had one other external evaluation of the Calendar and the Faculty Development Program. In addition, the Board itself has funded an evaluation of faculty development. Three evaluations, all substantial, completed in fourteen years. The evaluations have all been positive. The important point, however, is that the evaluations have been done.

To not evaluate intrapreneurial change is to invite trouble.

There must be visible outcomes of intrapreneurship. Data speaking to the quality of the intrapreneurial product are necessary. New faculty wonder if there are data to support this program they like so much and want to see continue. And with an eye to the future, data are important in maintaining the funding level, autonomy, and empowerment found in the program. This is the efficiency side of Faculty Development and intrapreneurship in general.

From another perspective the evaluations have been extended searches for feedback and ideas. They have served not only to protect the program and its culture but have helped them grow.

Several years after the first faculty projects were funded, it came time to deal with individual peers who, for one reason or another, had not filed their required final reports. The Board created a "past due" status. Faculty in past due status could not receive any more Board funds until they submitted satisfactory final reports for their projects. Additionally, the Board appealed to the Deans and received their cooperation in applying College sanctions on "past due" faculty. In most cases faculty who are "past due" cannot receive college travel monies or money to teach summer school. By responding to this problem, the group identity of the Board was reinforced. And each individual within the group saw the benefits of having a strong group identity to absorb the tension that such a professional reprimand always generated.

The Need to Take Risks

Eventually, the culture also took risks. Two art projects were supported. It was important that the culture of the Board recognize all experts in whatever disciplines. Those in the arts and music are often poorly understood by their "nonartistic" academic colleagues. One artist (international in reputation) was himself taking large risks in attempting to make ceramics larger than he ever had before. The ceramics kept breaking and the Development Board received no product. But the artist had learned a great deal. This artist recently told one of the authors that he is still learning about the technology of working with

clay bodies in inclement Wisconsin climates. His artistic learning, in this area, is ongoing eight years after his initial funding.

On another occasion, an artist created an earth sculpture which
was comprised of a series of "mounds" intersected by narrow
concrete paths. The vegetation on the mounds became un-
sightly, difficult to care for by building and grounds personnel.
The mounds became an object of ridicule and the center of much
controversy on campus. The Development Board stood by its
decision to fund the artist, believing that it must support all of
its colleagues who have meritorious ideas. In all these decisions the Board demonstrated initiative and flexibility which
came from a strong procedural and cultural base.

The Need for Succession

After five years the senior administrator stepped down as
Board Chair, but remained on the Board. While still a Board
member, he had the opportunity to work with two faculty Board
chairs. He began to attend meetings somewhat less frequently,
his first "real" absences in seven years. The Board began to
separate from him, looking to him for support and guidance
less frequently. After nine years of service he left the Board.
The culture was now free-standing. The first faculty chair took
over without the presence of the Development Board founder.
This new faculty chair had been on the Board for seven years.
The culture was maintained; it is an excellent example of the
importance of succession in establishment of culture.

CONCLUDING THOUGHTS

To establish a new culture, especially when there are strong
competing values and beliefs which have a long history in an
organization, requires that the new subunit be "firmly" established and planted before the intrapreneur (in this case the senior administrator who oversaw Faculty Development) starts to
stress and bend it. To build culture takes a very long time perspective. It assumes that people will have to live together for a
long time, and that the group will stand within the larger or-

ganization for a long time. Our experiences support the conclusion that new cultures can be placed and survive in a public organization. What is needed is competence in leadership, commitment of organizational members, and enough time (years) to get the job done.

The leadership in our case was the senior administrator who was able to articulate a vision and enforce it (Schein, 1985a). He understood the competing cultures he would confront and could solidify new assumptions. He did whatever had to be done to "train" a group of faculty in expert power and decision-making. In doing this he emphasized both the "know-why" and the "know-how" (Bennis and Nanus, 1985). This strong initial shaping force of a leader's personality is necessary if a culture is to grow and bloom. The result for the Development Board was a collegial social architecture.

At our University a strategy for cultural longevity worked. Expert power remains as a culture within the Faculty Development Board. But this culture has not spread widely to other forums and groups within the institution. Does this mean that the intrapreneurial effort is any less a success? We do not think so. The expert culture still exists as a model of how the University could function if others want to observe and take advantage of its decision-making technology, values, and world assumptions. Within the expert power culture is the assumption that people can honestly confront each other. This conflicts with a wider organizational culture that people should be nice to each other, meeting in calm without affect.

Faculty Development is also one of the few areas of empowerment; in many other parts of the organization power is legitimate. The expert culture helps support faculty who do not believe that being a typical regional university is good enough. Its communication is open versus a more closed communication culture throughout the institution. As a matter of fact, communication and meeting face to face is so much a part of the Board's culture that when discussions of electronic mail arose the Board rejected its use. The technology violated the culture of the Board; people wanted to get together for meetings. Encapsulated in Faculty Development is a model of how an entire academic institution could perform for the better. The culture has survived. Faculty Development is one place in the institution prepared to meet an uncertain future with vitality.

The expert culture described in this chapter is one of looking inward to the needs of the University's faculty, not outward to government affairs (Davis, 1985). As such it serves to provide balance to the chief executive officer and others who must heed the state system's beck and call. An inward-focused expert culture is not only possible, therefore, in a public university, it may be a necessity if such institutions are to be quality academic organizations.

Chapter 12
Wisdom

As the years pass, and the intrapreneurial changes become more and more the status quo, the need exists to write down our collective understanding of what was accomplished at the University. The journey and its accomplishments take on deeper meaning if we can capture the essence of the shared intrapreneurial experiences. Saga is a useful description and metaphor for this since it incorporates both a rational description and an affective devotion. As authors we believe and feel strongly about the Calendar, our registration system, and faculty development. The use of timekeeping as technology has a certain beauty for us. We have shared in watching these grow and have committed time and energy to them. What we describe is a special history with special meaning.

In this chapter we share with the reader that which we view as most important in our efforts and commitment. We know that what we share as a "sense of the unique" (Clark, 1975) is probably not so unique at all; others have been, in their own way, on the same journey. But it is still important that we write down that which makes the most sense to us about this particular example of academic intrapreneurship and its management. By doing so, it may become a valuable resource not only for members of our own organization but members in other organizations as well. In essence, we are writing about the capacity of a university to enhance the lives of its participants.

COMMITMENT AND COMMUNITY

We learned first hand that intrapreneurial work requires leadership and empowerment. But these are not ends in themselves. The barometer of whether one is successful in empowering and moving toward a desired future is the formation and maintenance of commitment, in this case by faculty in our University. What Kanter (1972) describes as the soul of communes and utopias is also the heart of intrapreneurship. The water which keeps the mill wheel turning is commitment (not coercion), collective feelings which serve as motivation and underlie the sweat equity so necessary for any group to succeed.

Talks of tenure layoffs and budget payback are antithetical to academic work. The faculty at our University were fleeing from problems and a reality with which they did not want to cope. The Chancellor's goal was a path which, if traveled, would do away with the painful reality of organizational dysfunction. He was trying to ensure the welfare of all faculty by ending tenure layoffs. The intrapreneurship had great meaning because all events had a purpose in terms of the beliefs and values of the faculty. The crisis was a serious one. The faculty knew something had to be done so that their value of tenure and beliefs in an academic life could be reaffirmed. It was a case of "the 'me' spirit . . . subordinated to the 'we' spirit" (Kanter, 1972, p. 41). It was a reality to which faculty could commit and attach.

A sense of community is enhanced when distinctions between people are erased or eased. The value of interactions, face-to-face meetings, and processes or mechanisms which counteract isolation, loneliness, and fragmentation cannot be underestimated. The number of ad hoc committees, the peril facing the University, shared written communications (e.g., the Calendar Papers), the few months in which to reach a solution, and the Chancellor's personal style all brought people together.

Intrapreneurship must deal people in and cannot deal them

out. People must be invested in the change; they must own it and find it rewarding. Once faculty made such a moral commitment to Faculty Development and other changes at the University, they gained purpose, direction, and the meaning they were seeking. Their academic identity was strengthened. The intrapreneurship helped detach them from the old organization with its problems and identity and set the stage for the next Chancellor to attach the faculty to a new organization with a new identity. The way this happened is all very beautiful and logical from a commitment perspective.

Other elements of community—and thus of commitment—are joy, celebration, and fun. The intrapreneurial Chancellor had a sense of fun and whimsy. This trickled down into the organization. People were under threat and working hard. He gave them permission to play while on organization time.

One outcome of the intrapreneurship, and one reason the University still has Calendar, registration, and faculty development, is that once the chaos had receded faculty were highly conscious of themselves as a community. They were very aware of what had transpired at the University. A sense of "communion" (collective unity) existed for many of the faculty. Oshkosh was different. It had been through a lot and had survived. What faculty had valued had come to pass; the University was closer to how the faculty wanted it to be.

Commitment is solidified when members in a group sacrifice. In order to gain, there must be something lost. Oshkosh faculty sacrificed much. They spent a great deal of time working on Calendar Papers and the intrapreneurial effort. They gave up power when on-line registration began. They lost the ability to control which students entered and did not enter their classes. They sacrificed monetary gain, since payment for extra work was less than at sister UW institutions. These sacrifices cemented commitment to the changes.

The concept of commitment and community clarifies the dangers which threaten the intrapreneurial products. New faculty, hired since 1977, have not sacrificed like their longer tenured colleagues. New faculty also may not have an identity with the organization nor a sense of its past and the journey it has made. The Calendar and faculty development are the status quo for the more recently hired faculty and administrators. Without a commitment to these ideas they may be more likely to negotiate them away for other values or products they desire. Thus, those with such a commitment and those without one may eventually come into conflict, as pressures are built up, and tensions created. As the organization ages, and more years pass since the intrapreneurship, the search for a common community will become fragmented unless leadership and vision give a common quest for direction and purpose.

EFFICIENCY AND EFFECTIVENESS

Successful intrapreneurship demands *both* efficiency and effectiveness. Registration, the Calendar, and faculty development were instituted because they were good ideas. But effectiveness is not enough. Good ideas must be manageable. On-line registration required thousands of hours of programming mainframe computers and close attention to a thousand unexpected problems. Allowing faculty to use Time creatively required the creation of a new technology. A new personnel data base had to be instituted. Without this the overhead to run faculty development and the faculty side of the Calendar would have been too costly; the good ideas would have died in paperwork and error.

But efficiency and effectiveness have not come easily. It has been difficult to manage the Calendar.

The Calendar was a hybrid of an idea and a working environment, a cross between a mechanic's love of systematic invention and an innocently dynamic environment that was changing and reforming itself on an almost daily basis. . . . The Calender's secret was tied to blinding speed and self-confident aggressiveness. . . . The essential barrier to most faculty (as well as the essential magnetism to some) was an epistemological barrier, a total inability to regard time as their own resource rather than their own master. The leaders could promise but the followers could not believe. . . . Only the most hypersensitive and intuitive were able to appreciate the Calendar's allure. (Wood, 1977, pp. 1–3)

Nevertheless, managing faculty development has proved to be possible and successful, promoting growth and development while at the same time remaining accountable (to faculty, management, and UW System). The program must be effective *and* be able to stand up to a detailed audit (the "tight" side of loose–tight). Only by careful management has the program been able to supply supportive data to maintain its budget, and thus, its place in the University. Only by being efficient, understanding its budget, planning, and paying attention to details (functions in which faculty usually do not involve themselves) has the development board been able to serve the faculty as a whole.

Attention to both effectiveness and efficiency is an example of vision with reality. Ideas, leadership, and empowerment must be doable. There must be ways by which an organization can make ideas work.

"WHY NOT?"

Intrapreneurship demands an empowering of people. There is simply too much work to be done, too much ambiguity, and too much at stake not to trust others. But while empowerment sounds simple, it is not. If we learned anything it is that one must always ask *"Why Not?"* The key is to avoid the trap of asking "Why?" People become tired, deadlines are omnipresent, there are pressures to succeed and to get on with the work. There is even more of a temptation to become traditional and nontrustful once intrapreneurship is over. The Faculty Development Board has maintained a culture of always asking, "Why not?" Why not trust a faculty and take a risk with funding? Why not fund a proposal which asks for something new and different?

It is hard to ask "Why not?" Faculty, as much as any group, can be confrontive and manipulative. The natural predilection is to rein in control and creativity. To treat faculty in a fair, effective, patient, and trustful manner, it helps to realize that "We all manipulate."

A culture of "why not" has to take place within a loose–tight framework. Not everything is fair game. The tight part of faculty development is the vision of professional development of faculty. The loose part is responding to faculty positively within this vision. Thus, if errors are made in faculty development they are made on the side of empowerment, on the side of supporting faculty rather then denying them funding, and on the side of trusting people until proven otherwise.

Trusting people until proven otherwise is especially relevant in an academic setting. Reputation is a valuable commodity in a college or university. Faculty will strive for a positive reputation, be concerned when they do not have one, and fight with others when they feel their reputations are unfairly portrayed. Reputation is terribly important. A concern with reputation is a strong control on inappropriate behaviors and assists in maintaining a trusting culture.

RELENTLESS DEDICATION

Intrapreneurship demands relentless dedication. It is like an always flowing river. There is always something to do, people with whom to meet, and more to do than can reasonably get done. An intrapreneur cannot pick up and leave or give up because he or she feels like it. Time off or fun is necessary but only because it will recharge the batteries and lead to more productive work. Empowerment helps with part of this role overload. But there are other mechanisms which also help.

One of these is to *codify—always write it down*. One way of surviving during an intrapreneurial effort is to define reality and know what universe one is working in day to day. The Calendar Papers are one such example. In seventy-five days, thirteen Calendar Papers were written which defined the parameters of the intrapreneurship. Two months later, over the course of sixty-five days, five Faculty Development Papers were also written. These are still the bible of the Calendar change and faculty development, fourteen years later! By having a written source of the ideas, rules, trade-offs, and deals which can be inspected, read, and reread, all the loose ends are tied up as much as possible.

Committing to written form what has been loose and oral has other advantages. The process of writing such documents assists various constituencies to compromise, to interact, and to own the final product. Written form also is structured and "real." It allows months of intrapreneurship to be put in one place and is the springboard for further intrapreneurial work. Effectiveness issues can be clearly spelled out. What is tight becomes tighter. Efficiency issues also can be attended to.

One last advantage of codifying is that it differentiates between activity that is "tinkering" and activity that is "careful attention" to efficiency. We advise to "tinker not." Once ideas are set, leave them alone. Written documents which capture purpose, issues, vision, and mission can serve as valuable archives—as resources for good "reality testing" and decision-making.

One way to find out, or to reaffirm, which ideas are integral to an organization is to go back to the written intrapreneurial documents. Once these are known and one's memory refreshed, it becomes clear what is process and what is commandment.

For example, the faculty development program has seen many changes. New components have been instituted and accounting practices have been improved. The motto of the Faculty Development Board, under the rubric of both efficiency and relentless dedication, is that "if it ain't broke, pay attention to it." But the ideas integral to the program have been left alone. The program serves the professional development of faculty in their academic and professional work. Risk taking, opportunity, and quality scholarship are valued.

A last part of relentless dedication is to *always follow through*. Intrapreneurship is only as good as its product (idea) and its people. And these people are only as good as their honesty, trustworthiness, and integrity. For intrapreneurs to be able to provide leadership, their words must be good. The way of ensuring this is to always follow through on what is promised and what is done. If intrapreneurs say something, they had better do it. This is one way commitment is generated. Passion in the service of an idea must be coupled with an intense attention to detail. This does not mean that an intrapreneur can always succeed and can always deliver what is promised. But good intrapreneurs keep track of their transactions and let people know as soon as possible about decisions and courses of action, even if the answer is "no."

While this is important in the intrapreneurial process, it is especially important to solidification of an intrapreneurial project once it has a product to be managed. The real worth of the Faculty Development Board and the singular behavior which allowed it to gain the faculty's trust was that the program *served* faculty. It always followed through, quickly, immediately, and as promised. There were timely decisions for faculty, *always*. The Board attended to its faculty customers.

Decisions were also made correctly. Timeliness is no good if the response is ill conceived. In order to be timely the Board had to work extremely hard. Such commitment is necessary. Faculty dreams and opportunities do not arise only in confluence with an academic schedule. Ideas are the most valuable currency in a college or university. They are "hot" property to a faculty. Faculty who want feedback on funding requests or are seeking information should receive it immediately. There is no substitute for relentless dedication in the service of intrapreneurship.

TRUST

Trust is all-important. Once trust is lost the chances for intrapreneurial success diminish greatly. There are ways to maximize trust. We have already described several ways: being true to one's word; providing quick, quality responses to queries; and following through. Let us offer two more mechanisms for maximizing trust.

No Inside Trading

Members of an intrapreneurial team may have information, or contact with important organizational members, or resources which are not available to the general employee. These valuable commodities must be used to further chances of intrapreneurial success. One must never feather one's own nest. There can be no inside trading as a result of intrapreneurship.

Intrapreneurs cannot be perceived as benefiting from their positions except as formal organizational reward systems treat them.

This is equally true in managing intrapreneurial products. The Faculty Development Board succeeds and generates trust, in part, because it has a culture of no inside trading. The Board obviously has much information about the reasoning behind criteria for successful proposals. It knows how much budget it has and where it would like these monies spent. Board members have ample opportunity to lobby their Board colleagues on proposals they themselves have submitted. They have equal opportunity to do so for proposals colleagues submit.

But the culture of the board does not condone this behavior. Some board members have chosen not to submit any proposals themselves while serving on the Board! Others abstain on votes which involve their colleagues or units. In one case two faculty voted in the minority ("yes") for a fairly weak and subsequently rejected proposal from a full professor in their college. One of these board members must have felt the inappropriateness of his vote and made a comment directly after the decision at the meeting: "Maybe I should have abstained." Without a word said to him directly, he felt the culture against inside trading acting on him.

Don't Fight In Public. Pettiness Does Not Count

Another method of generating trust is to keep a program focused on its goals. Any intrapreneurial project or product which reaches production and "sticks," that is, is a success, will have more going for it than against it. As such there is little purpose in publicly taking people to task. The urge to do so is strong, however. There are certain faculty, for example, who have behaved in ways that the Faculty Development Board felt a strong pull to reprimand. Part of the responsibility of such a Board is to deal with irritating constituents with grace and fairness.

There is almost no situation in which going public with a battle or name calling can be productive in an intrapreneurial effort. Trust is gained by being professional and handling difficulties in a problem-solving mode.

WHAT IS, IS

Sometimes the search for cause and reason overlooks the obvious and it is in the latter where the truth may be found. Some things just are. Let us offer two examples of truth in simple form.

You Can't Change Something Without Changing It

Intrapreneurship is a process of change. But as a University Calendar or registration is changed there are many questions of why things are being done the way they are. The answer is that *something cannot be changed without making it different*. Moving across discontinuity from one S-curve to another demands that this be so. A good intrapreneur has to be able to see how things will be different.

Communicating that things cannot be changed without being changed makes clear to organizational members why there is so much chaos, creativity, ambiguity, and newness surrounding an intrapreneurial effort.

You Can't Give Up Control Without Giving Up Control

Intrapreneurship requires empowerment, new processes, and a vision of a new future. But empowerment, which requires much more than delegating, is a process of giving up control. What is held tight is the vision, the percepts, or the effectiveness issues which drive the change. All else is empowered to others. The intrapreneurial team members will do it their way. The temptation is to give up control without giving up control. It cannot be done. Such an approach is tokenism and misused power in the guise of empowerment and trust.

There was no way at our University to empower faculty to be responsible for, and provide leadership for, faculty development without giving them control over the monies, the ideas, and the process. One cannot delegate autonomy. Either the faculty is responsible for its development, or it is not.

YOU CANNOT BE A BLEEDING HEART AND AN INTRAPRENEUR

There are always losers. People are always affected by change, some positively, some negatively. Intrapreneurs have to get on with their work. A sensitivity to the individual plight of each organization's employee is not possible. Do not misunderstand us. Intrapreneurs need empathy, relationships, sympathy, and caring. But what is good for the organization is not always good for each of its people. In this case the whole is greater than the sum of its parts.

For those faculty at UW–Oshkosh who always taught summer school for additional compensation, and wanted to do this in the future, the new financial arrangements hurt. For those faculty who had spent long hours and much deliberation in teaching the best seventeen-week course they could, the new Calendar forced them to do much hard work in order to redo their courses to fit a fourteen-week semester. For those faculty who valued or prized the traditional registration process, the new registration technology allowed them to advise students but not to determine in many cases who entered their classes.

ACADEMIA IS NOT UNIQUE

Nothing that we experienced, observed, or did leads us to believe that academic organizations are in any major way different from any other organization when it comes to intrapreneurship. The University was able to move quickly when it had to. Faculty governance did not change the intrapreneurial process one iota. There are no special problems we can conceptualize which makes intrapreneurship more difficult than in other organizations. It is that simple.

VISION IS NOT NECESSARY

The intrapreneurial Chancellor did not have a clear, articulated vision of the organization s future, yet he was successful in the process of instituting change. He painted a canvas with gray and black, doom and gloom. He offered no clear alternative but to lead the faculty away from the pits of Oshkosh damnation. Despite the literature's emphasis on vision as a vehicle for successful intrapreneurship, it is not an absolutely necessary ingredient.

One can lead either by a vision or a *direction*. For some organizations, the latter is what happens. They do not know exactly where they are going, but they know which direction they are moving in! The intrapreneurial Chancellor wanted to move toward continuous Time. He saw this as a way to be able to manage resources more effectively. He believed that students needed this. He also saw this as the proper direction for professional development. And he wanted to move toward a more playful environment. But he had no vision of any of this. It was sufficient to know in which direction to move.

FAILURES WILL OCCUR

Wisdom is not gained by success alone. As a matter of fact, getting "beat up" a little bit (or a lot) gets people's attention and seasons them for future opportunities and intrapreneurship. One cannot be a good intrapreneur without failing.

The Oshkosh Calendar, at a manifest level, is a relative failure. Few faculty have used it for really innovative management of time. As we have written, this may be due to the fact that time management technologies were never fully developed. While the Calendar permits innovation, it has not fostered innovative programs or faculty activity at a level or in ways which were hoped for. It has not attracted nor generated the number of part-time, older, or working students it was promised to recruit. As a matter of fact, the new semester system itself probably had little overtly to do with the recent resurgence of the University's enrollment. But the process of Calendar reform *was* a resounding success as a tool in unfreezing the organization, empowering the faculty, instituting faculty development, and modernizing registration and the faculty personnel data base. What is seen as failure may not be so.

Faculty Development, too, has known its failures in strategy and implementation. One component called "University Needs" had great potential for assisting the organization to remain intrapreneurial. The idea behind this component is an interesting one: Any faculty or administrator could suggest a perceived University need to the Faculty Development Board, which would then publish a campuswide request for proposals aimed at addressing this University Need. This empowers the faculty both to have its ideas heard and to assist in problem solution in sevice of the organization. It has been used a dozen times in as many years, no more. The faculty have not been interested in the component. The problem is that the currency of faculty is ideas and, the way the Needs component is structured, one gives away one's ideas for free. The component would be much more intrapreneurial and successful, we believe, if the faculty who identify a problem (or need) could be funded to attack the problem without an organizationwide call for proposals. This is very much a venture capital model: One earns funds to solve problems. The more problems one correctly perceives, or the more motivated one is to be an intrapreneur or assist the organization, the more one can establish and carry out needs projects.

A third failure lies in the area of culture. Expert power was established for faculty as a basic assumption of how faculty would make decisions. Other potentials of the intrapreneurship's influence on organizational culture did not eventuate. An openness to innovation, technology, risk taking, and opportunity has not prevailed. Once the crisis was past, a more conservative approach to problem solving took hold. It is difficult to manage a culture when leaders change in an organization. New styles of management and different goals drive different cultures. Will the organization encounter problems which force it to make further use of an expert power strategy or new technology? We do not know.

A fourth failure was in lack of follow-through, both technically and with passion, on use of the Calendar for innovative curricula and teaching. There was no special group of faculty (in parallel to the Faculty Development Board) formally empowered to facilitate this. There was no administrator passionately committed to an expert decision-making culture in relationship to curriculum. Eventually, the technology of the Calendar ground to a halt. It would have taken great creative effort to maintain the viability of an unlimited number of new teaching possibilities. The idea was a good one which never materialized. We failed to make a successful leap from one curricular and teaching S-curve to another.

Last is the issue of saga (Clark, 1975). No organizational saga has developed from the intrapreneurial work. What our University experienced had the potential to generate loyalty, trust, communication, cooperation, and a collective understanding of the unique experiences of the faculty. Faculty Development is the closest the organization has come to keeping hold of the specialness of the intrapreneurial years.

The potential existed for the faculty to grab hold of its performance and place, and affectively and rationally commit to a deep meaningful stream of shared experience. Most faculty in the organization really do not know what took place in the mid-1970s, and if they do, it has not led to a continued feeling of special place or special shared history among them. What was originally "strong purpose" no longer is a means of unity; the intrapreneurship no longer deeply commits faculty to the University. This failure in culture could be reversed, but only by a new leader with vision using the products of the intrapreneurial work. We fear that time is running out. The intrapreneurship generated strong purpose and special effort which is becoming past history without special meaning. The faculty cadre of true believers is less and less visible. The number of faculty with a living memory of the intrapreneurship continues to dwindle. There is no ideology around which history can be placed. A rare opportunity (rare, in general, and even more so because of the organization's size and public status) for unparalleled meaning and unity may have been lost.

PART V

THE FUTURE

Chapter 13
The Transpreneurial Organization

Where is a college or university to start? What is the vision for those interested in moving to an intrapreneurial environment? This chapter provides this vision. We call it the *Transpreneurial Organization*. It is a vision of an academic institution which pays attention to its people and establishes a climate and culture of great value in and of itself, *regardless of whether intrapreneurship is widely practiced!*

Large intrapreneurial changes in education are usually crisis-driven. Institutions without crisis may not choose to be intrapreneurial in their focus. We hold that academic institutions initially need to become more effective, more efficient, and more vital. A passion in the service of education is necessary. This initial organizational vision incorporates most of the dimensions relevant to intrapreneurship without demanding intrapreneurship per se. Concepts such as leadership, empowerment, culture, experimentation, rewards, opportunity, and people have great meaning in the service of any successful college or university. It is by these mechanisms that groups can get work done without coercion and build meaningful relationships between group members. The problem to be solved is one of commitment—commitment by an institution to a meaningful role in higher education and commitment of its members to the institution.

Colleges and universities initially must strive to be Transpreneurial Organizations. This view of organizations is one that spans organizational types. Entrepreneurial organizations are those which value and pursue new ventures. New projects and ventures developed and brought to fruition within an organization is the intrapreneurial process. The intrapreneurial organization values exploration, development, creativity, pathfinding (Leavitt, 1987), and cultures, all of which are related to major flexibility and change within an institution.

We use the term transpreneurial from the perspective of a pulling together of an organization's structure, strategy, systems, and vision such that the organizational culture reflects the importance (as basic values) of trust and integrity, empowerment, and people. Thus, an academic institution can be very transpreneurial even with a past history of few new programs or new ventures, and little if any practice of intrapreneurship. We see this as the organizational style of choice for institutions of higher education.

The Transpreneurial Organization is especially relevant for academic institutions. The amount of intrapreneurship in which colleges and universities will engage varies enormously. But all need to empower their people, ask and answer effectiveness questions, and strive to offer a quality product which people value. Academic organizations for the most part cannot and do not strengthen themselves by either merger or acquisition. They are what they are. Their only road to success is internal strength. Becoming transpreneurial is a way of building this strength.

Transpreneurial Organizations are ones in which the emperor has no clothes on. All employees are free to " . . . ask innocently optimistic questions equivalent to those asked by small children; questions like 'What shall we do today?' " (Leavitt, 1987, p. 53). Transpreneurial Organizations value people and their ideas.

Empowering people and being transpreneurial does not mean, however, that all people are treated the same. Transpreneurial organizations are not "levelers," as are many academic institutions. Leveling in academia is an insidious process which, in the name of academic community or common identity, treats everyone the same, regardless of productivity, quality, or contribution. Transpreneurial Universities reward, recognize, and value those who make genuine contributions, whether in the classroom or to organizational process and functioning.

Transpreneurial Organizations have the challenge of really treating people as important resources. One approach to this is the IBM idea of keeping internal customers satisfied (Labovitz, 1987). Internal customers are whoever your work moves to next. For example, the internal customers for academic deans would be department chairpersons, faculty, academic staff, or students; for chairpersons they would be faculty; for upper-level administrators, they would be academic staff, faculty, and so on. Serving internal customers requires cooperation and exploration of interdependent ties within an organization. Everyone must work together. Since there is no dollar cost to this, there is no visible barrier to its adaptation within academic organizations.

As part of valuing people, Transpreneurial Organizations adopt an ethic of interdependence (Drucker, 1985b). This is an Oriental Confucian set of ethics which recognize that "right behavior . . . is that individual behavior which is truly appropriate to the specific relationship of mutual dependence because it optimizes benefits for both parties" (Drucker, 1985b, p. 249). Ethical behavior supports and creates trust and harmony, not exploitation and manipulation. Integrity of relationships must be maintained. The ethic of interdependency supports the basic suppositions and values on which a Transpreneurial Organization is constructed. "[I]nterdependence demands equality of obligations" (Drucker, 1985b, p. 251). People are obligated to provide what others need in order to help them to achieve the goals of the organization. This is not an ethic in which one side has obligations and the other side rights. Faculty and academic management under this ethical model have obligations both to each other and to the goals of their college and university (students, research, service, or the pursuit of truth).

Transpreneurial Organizations are learning environments which value opportunity and sponsors; they are not failure-averse. They allow people to stick with good ideas over time. They have a tolerance for risk and failure. They place high esteem on value and good ideas. They disdain turf issues. They divest themselves of failures and are not afraid to make decisions. Their cultures are productive.

A Transpreneurial Organization, compared to a more traditional organization, gives more encouragement to new ideas and waits longer before turning off these new ideas. In this way, a Transpreneurial Organization facilitates the intrapreneurial process. In striving to achieve and maintain a Transpreneurial environment, it is our hypothesis that intrapreneurship becomes more likely to occur and to be successful when it does. Dedicated people must be allowed to work on the things in which they believe.

Transpreneurial Organizations take advantage of intrapreneurs if they are present. Information (one part of power) exists for everyone at all levels of the institution. The traditional, segmented, bureaucratic university would no longer be highly valued. Being steady on course when the ship is heading for the rocks does not make sense.

The primary problem in academic institutions is not the blocking of vision but the blocking of action. A Transpreneurial Institution would be very sensitive to this problem.

Only when people with proven performance capacity have been assigned to a project, supplied with the tools, the money, and the information they need to do the work, and given clear and unambiguous deadlines—only then do we have a plan. Until then, we have "good intentions," and what those are good for, everybody knows. (Drucker, 1985a, pp. 154–155)

By valuing and emphasizing people, their empowerment, trust, and integrity, and by maintaining a positive culture oriented toward a vital future (all of which can exist without major intrapreneurship present) the Transpreneurial Organization emphasizes "freedom factors" (Pinchot, 1985). These factors include allowing people to self-select themselves for tasks, allowing people to stick with tasks once implemented, allowing people to make decisions, having a way to get people some power (resources, information, and support), and valuing the small and beautiful, not only the home run. In other words: Is there freedom to move the institution forward?

Academic institutions need to value people in their day-to-day traditional activities. The organization can be conservative in its strategies and shun intrapreneurship. Its niches can be so successful that it does not need to value change and intrapreneurs. But the organization still needs to be transpreneurial.

The Transpreneurial University follows through on commitment, values, vision, and people. It does not strive to be all things to all people. Through the use of transpreneurial concepts and ideas, institutions can provide a strong education despite falling resources and other problems. A lack of resources is not viewed as a reason or excuse for not getting the job done. Regional universities and other public institutions would be well served with a problem-solving, transpreneurial model of functioning.

The Transpreneurial Organization is flexible and moves toward new assumptions of its goals and how to meet them. New ideas which have value are kept alive because the institutional environment is a nurturing one. The environment has the leadership to assist people make the institution's vision a reality. Transpreneurial Organizations believe people can contribute, care about their efforts, and have a culture of pride. People, climate, and structure are what is important, not resources per se.

Transpreneurial Organizations represent a new management strategy. Intrapreneurial organizations represent a second new management strategy. The synergy of the two has the potential to greatly assist academe. Paying attention to a thousand little things, while at the same time attending to the grand issues, is attainable in a Transpreneurial Organization.

Chapter 14
The Future

Academic institutions must have a thorough self-understanding of their strategies, missions, and goals. It is this understanding which precedes and sets the stage for productivity, vitality, and effectiveness approaches aimed at strengthening any institution of higher education. Facing the future means asking hard but relevant questions. The purpose of a transpreneurial structure and the process of intrapreneurship are to help an institution meet the future successfully.

Colleges and universities cannot best serve their constituents by only doing more of the same. A strategy of embracing and adopting the status quo will take these institutions only so far.

Adaptation of the transpreneurial philosophy sets the stage and primes the pump. It develops and/or maintains an enterprise in which people are valued and are free to contribute to their institution's goals and missions. Being transpreneurial allows the well water of ideas and effort to flow freely. And when concerted, focused change is needed, intrapreneurial efforts will be best carried out in a transpreneurial climate and culture.

INTRAPRENEURIAL CHALLENGES

The most important challenge facing colleges and universities in the years ahead is the need to adopt and develop new programs, products, and technologies which we cannot even conceptualize today. If procrastination is opportunity's natural assassin (Kiam, 1986), it can be overcome. If new ventures are to have any chance of being succesfully integrated into a curriculum, and if program units are to have success in maintaining or increasing resources to support these efforts, transpreneurial beliefs and intrapreneurship will surely come into play.

A second challenge for colleges and universities attempting to position for a vital future is the identification of their organizational structure and strategic type. Some will implement organizational audits (Miles and Snow, 1978; Wheelen and Hunger, 1984) to accomplish this task. The critical question here is whether these institutions are Reactor, Defender, Analyzer, or Prospector, and the determination of whether this is how they want to be. Issues of rewards, controls, and personnel will have to be confronted. A transpreneurial climate and culture which facilitates but does not necessitate intrapreneurial work would help an institution adopt and/or maintain a structure congruent with its strategy, vision, and goals for the future.

Related to structure and strategic type is the issue of leadership and culture. How does a transpreneurial culture become instituted? Who provides the passion and who provides the wisdom? How do academic institutions gain mission statements which are useful? Who maintains cultures which are good for the organization and how do outdated cultures get changed? The answer, once again, is the intrapreneur.

At the most basic level, but most importantly, is the quality, excitement, and drama of what transpires in classrooms across the country. "There is no substitute for providing courses and classroom experiences that are stimulating and worthwhile to the students who take them" (Dressel, 1987, p. 103). Regardless of resources and whether a college or university is public or private, the issue is one of educating students well.

A quality curriculum appears static from a distance but is not. Changes and tinkering are always ongoing. And as some of these alterations become larger and more serious, such as new general education requirements, or integrated freshman studies, or new requirements for graduation in the liberal arts, someone will have to shepherd these proposals and changes through the academic institution labyrinth of decision-making to a positive conclusion. We argue that the shepherd in many cases will be an intrapreneur.

Both classroom learning and teaching and a meaningful curriculum are tied in many institutions to the undergraduate experience they offer their students. It is this undergraduate experience which Boyer (1987) has described in such richness and detail. Everything which comprises the undergraduate experience, from recruitment of students, orientation once they arrive at campus, language, general education, specialization (the major), faculty, creativity, resources, campus life, extending the campus into the community, managing all of this, and measuring the outcomes, is grist for the intrapreneur's mill.

Bowen (1982), five years earlier than Boyer, argued for a vision of a nation of educated people with a special attention to American youth. These individuals would be educated for values and the international world in which we now all live. Bowen's nation of educated people required focus and emphasis on the Baccalaureate degree and the course of study leading to this degree. His was a vision of the well-educated person and of our society and the people living in it. Surely these are lofty and noble causes. But how does such a vision become a reality? We believe the answer is one campus at a time. Visions come true by one intrapreneur at a time working to make them real.

If Bowen's (1982) vision of a nation of educated people is to be the path of destiny (Miller, 1988) for colleges and universities, then they must be prepared to respond to three issues of such magnitude which affect all of us. These include the worldwide technology revolution, changing values in our society and world, and a global economy. Our institutions of higher education cannot ignore these issues and the changes they portend for our future. In fact they must understand them, respond to them in their research and curriculum, and educate their students about them. All of this implies change, flexibility, and a transpreneurial and intrapreneurial perspective.

Another area of important challenge and concern in our society and to our institutions of higher education is the life-long student and the older student in general. Their presence on campus is likely to increase as our society ages and as an emphasis on being educated continues. Teaching and working with the older student can be exciting, challenging, and fulfilling. But, again, there are issues of integrating "continuing education" into not only the structure of an academic organization but into the mind-set and souls of its faculty. How will changing values, demographics, and life-long education influence and be dealt with by colleges and universities?

An especially difficult and important problem is the recruitment and retention of minority students to our college and university campuses. At best, academic institutions have had limited success in this area. At the worst, the problem is still largely unsolved—the effort is a failure. Will society expect such institutions to devote more of their (limited) budgets in pursuit of this problem versus others?

If innovative (new technology) solutions to moral dilemmas are conceptualized, a transpreneurial philosophy and appreciation of intrapreneurship will best serve colleges and universities in their efforts. These will be some of the best ways for higher education to serve the disenfranchised and the disempowered, and to meet its commitments to people and to society.

The challenge is one of academia developing new technology and new products to improve the quality of higher education, however defined. Is there an academic parallel to corporate departments of research and development? How do we ensure that our future visionaries in academia, wherever we discover them, have a chance to speak, are heard, and can implement their ideas? And how do we maximize the probability that we will discover them in the first place? Clearly, a transpreneurial orientation toward academic functioning is one key.

Without the academic equivalent of Research and Development pushing new ideas, the pressure to evaluate the status quo and decide what is or is not worth keeping is lessened. There must be impetus to draw S-curves, calculate limits, and make use of this knowledge in strategy and decision-making. Higher education must stop starving tomorrow to feed yesterday.

THE PLACE FOR ACADEMIC INTRAPRENEURSHIP

Why are so many universities establishing entrepreneur centers to help business? Who helps academia? How do universities and colleges deal with their environments, needs, and programs?

Seib (1984) postulates two laws of "Acadynamics." The first law is that by the time educators recognize a problem it is probably beyond solution. The second law is that academic administrators call for financing and maintaining the status quo. If there is any truth in his reasoning that these two "laws" explain why reforms in higher education tend to be more cosmetic than cosmic, then intrapreneurship is one process to counter these strong "natural academic" forces and a transpreneurial structure one model to accomplish the same goal.

Colleges and universities cannot get where they need to go using only an efficiency model. Changes, both large and small, continue to be implemented in colleges and universities. Areas for intrapreneurship can be found everywhere. There are many intrapreneurial problems waiting for solutions at all universities. Academic problems continue year after year, sapping resources, time, and energy from more productive efforts.

The function of intrapreneurship is to get positive changes implemented. If intrapreneurship is not the process by which academic business gets done, what is the process—Incrementalism—forever? How can incrementalism be embraced for all solutions?

There is only one way to make innovation attractive to managers: a systematic policy of abandoning whatever is outworn, obsolete, no longer productive, as well as the mistakes, failures and misdirections of effort. Every three years or so, the enterprise must put every single product, process, technology, market, distributive channel, not to mention every single internal staff activity, on trial for its life. It must ask: Would we now go into this product, this market, this distributive channel, this technology today? If the answer is "No," one does not respond with, "Let's make another study." One asks, "What do we have to do to stop wasting resources on this product, this market, this distributive channel, this staff activity?" (Drucker, 1985a, p. 151)

It would be exciting if a college or university were to bring alive that which Drucker advocates. Where is our courage?

Structuring for intrapreneurs in a university setting is an interesting dilemma. The Defender side of the organization, tight and efficient, must be well run. The dilemma is how to choose wisely what types of resources and in what amounts these must be allocated to improve efficiency (good data for decision-making, adequate scanning, etc.) versus what must be allocated to effectiveness issues. A more serious problem is how an Analyzer or Defender university would nest in or create the looseness needed for intrapreneurship. Processes of empowerment, a belief in opportunity, and in keeping barriers down (not blocking visions or actions) would be helpful; these are transpreneurial. A culture of valuing people and good ideas is necessary; these also are transpreneurial. Realistic, well-thought-out missions are mandatory. If formal missions are not useful, the organization should adopt a "bootleg" mission, written to set the climate and guide behaviors for organizational members.

A massive change effort at the State University of New York at Buffalo failed (Bennis, 1975). But in listing major mistakes to be avoided when making future "great changes," Bennis focused on issues of integrity, history, climate, empowerment, vision within reality and detail, changing things by really changing them, and ownership of ideas. Intrapreneurial concepts had application and utility at Buffalo and at Oshkosh, and they have the potential to meaningfully guide and assist many colleges and universities into the future. It is one way to ensure that colleges and universities, as human organizations, survive and involve their members over a long period of time.

A transpreneurial orientation allows an institution to prepare to meet its future by maximizing its most important resource, its people. But institutions *must* follow through. They must do something. The case history we have written about Oshkosh shows how the intrapreneurs successfully established the "empowerment" support structures for the organizational effort.

We also believe that the enabling mechanisms of a Transpreneurial or Intrapreneurial Organization are best retained and

cles of a sleeping giant soon grow soft. The expert culture needs problems worthy of an expert community's attention.

FINAL THOUGHTS

Higher education makes up a large part of the third sector (nonbusiness, nongovernment) in our society. "The biggest infrastructure challenge for this country in the next decade is not the billions needed for railroads, highways, and energy. It is the American school system. . . . And it requires something far scarcer than money—thinking and risk-taking" (Drucker, 1985b, p. 138).

It is easier to create educational institutions than to close them down. "The result is that for untold years to come taxpayers will spend billions of dollars to maintain educational institutions that never should have been established in the first place. It is a terrible waste; but waste has a larger following than frugality—or common sense" (Yardley, 1987, p. 7). But this waste need not take place. Once established, academic institutions can be productive.

The data force us to accept Keller's (1983) thesis that the era of laissez-faire academic administration is over. Strategy and leadership are needed to move campuses into transpreneurial and intrapreneurial modes of being. Current realities must be faced by governing board members, administrators, and faculty. Educational organizations must prepare for the future. This is no time for rose-colored glasses. Faced at best with the challenge of maintaining a competetive edge, or at worst with the specter of decline, institutions must pull themselves together and institute substantial change. The Tooth Fairy Syndrome (Levine, 1979) will not prove true forever. Some academic institutions are going to have to survive based on their own efforts without hope of rescue from governmental or other benefactors.

There is no time for platitudes. It is a time for active involvement in the future of our own academic institutions. That is what transpreneurial organizations are all about: active involvement of empowered, trusted employees. The road to the strengthened through "practice" on real problems. The mus-

future is paved in intrapreneurship. We must make decisions and commit ourselves, consciously, to courses of action. To assist in this effort, institutions could consider having "intrapreneurs (or transpreneurs) in residence." These would be individuals who come to know the organization, its culture, people, and strategies, and are available to anyone who asks for brainstorming, consultation, and good talk.

Academia might do well to follow Wriston's (1959) advice and widen its contacts and outlook. Instead of taking the high moral road and waiting for corporate or organizational practices to be proven effective, college and university management must realize that such practices can be useful. Principle can still be put before expediency and scholars can still be valued as leaders and managers within academic settings. A commitment to higher education should drive college and university managers to good ideas, wherever they can find them.

Intrapreneurship as a process is a prescription for the better health of academe. It has been sufficiently described and used so that its value has been proven. It is an alternative to muddling through with an incrementalist approach to change. Intrapreneurship defines the dimensions and process necessary to maximize the probabilities of successful change. Academic institutions strive to produce educated people, not merely those who hold degrees. Intrapreneurship is one way in which higher education can deal continuously and flexibly with the continuous educational scenarios as they arise. "If every new idea must wait upon increased resources, so that it may be piled atop all the old procedures, the situation soon becomes hopeless" (Wriston, 1959, p. 169).

Transpreneurial and intrapreneurial—these are what we must strive to become.

PART VI

EPILOGUE

Chapter 15
Epilogue

The forty-two-month intrapreneurial effort ended with changes and growth in the University just begun—Paradox. The changes the Chancellor left behind were exhilarating but fragile; necessary changes, yet one series of choices out of many. The external crisis had been staved off. The organization needed time to manage the changes and get settled down. The faculty needed stability so it could focus once again on its work.

Where is the University now, over a decade after the intrapreneurship has drawn to a close? We are in a position of looking back over the past ten years (a relatively long time perspective) on the University performance. Much of the technology, culture, and structural changes put in place during the intrapreneurial years remain in the institution and have enabled it to be both more effective and more efficient than might have been the case without the change effort. The University's "profit" and niche are stronger because of the intrapreneurial work. The long-term return on the investment has been marked.

THE UNIVERSITY

The University has had one Chancellor since 1978—a Steward. This Chancellor has two important goals for the University, most accurately described as directions, not visions. He has urged that those who work at the University must "believe"; "We are not UW–Zero." How much easier a task had Oshkosh been named Athens, Wisconsin as was once proposed long ago! The leader's message of belief is one repeated endlessly. A new University logo, more academic and professional-looking, has been adopted.

The new Chancellor's second direction is that "We begin once again to act as other universities act." A University Convocation has been initiated as an annual event. Commencement, too, has been revitalized. An endowment and University Foundation are fully functional. The Teaching award for faculty has been strengthened and a "Professorship" program, the University's highest recognition for scholarship, is fully funded and annually awarded.

The fiscal situation has never been good. It took several years to fully pay back UW System the monies and faculty positions owed to it. Insufficient funds to support what needs to be done continues to be a chronic reality. But the budget problems of today do not affect the faculty nearly as much as what had gone before.

Our saga began with declining enrollments, tenure layoffs, and crisis. Now the higher the University raises its admission standards, the greater the number of students wanting to attend! We have too many students; they are like Tribbles in Star Trek. They are everywhere. Demography is destiny in higher education. The faculty is thankful for the students; it does not have to worry about the crises that are associated with falling enrollments. But, curiously, while the University has a great number of students, it receives less money per student; its revenues do not increase proportionally. Faculty workloads (e.g., size of classes) increase, and increase some more.

The "University of Alternatives" and open admissions have been eliminated. An honors program for students has been established. Faculty had wanted more attention to the University's best students and saw this as a way of attracting even more of them. We have (for us) a record number of National Merit Winners (second only to the state's flagship institution) and a record number of students in the top 25 percent of their high school classes.

The strategy of the present dominant coalition is clear, well focused, and very conscious. The University pays strong attention to efficiency. To obtain resources from UW System Administration, good data and their meaning are needed. We do this well, and the University is perceived highly by UW System Administration.

The University has received a glowing report for its North Central Accreditation. It is hoped that the UW System people read the document and understand how far the organization has come.

We strive to be an excellent regional University. The futurity of the organization is attended to, but conservatively. As such, this strategy lacks any special emphasis on intrapreneurial work, opportunity, or an appreciation for or reward for risk taking. There may be some missed boats (Dickson and Giglierano, 1986), risks never taken, and programs never begun.

As with any successful strategy, there have been costs. The pace of change is slow. For example, it took our College of Education three years to announce and tentatively put in place a new Teacher's Education program. A good intrapreneur with a good team could have delivered a higher quality product in less time.

Also, the organization has made little use of technology, limits, and discontinuity curves. The creative and productive use of Time as technology has not been supported by other leaps across S-curves or other reaching and surpassing of limits. For the most part we try to do better that which we have always done.

Effectiveness issues are seldom raised, but when they are it is difficult to meet identified needs. Several years ago the University set up an Institute to serve the microcomputer training needs of the region's business and industry. Despite much rhetoric from the state legislature and from UW System about the critical importance of higher education providing assistance to business, this Institute has been funded primarily through a reallocation of the University's base operating budget. It has not received any special funding from the state. A good idea, timely in its inception, and properly implemented, struggles for its life, its vitality impaired.

Another example illustrates a similar scenario. The College of Business Administration received permission from UW System to plan an entrepreneurship emphasis for undergraduates. There are more than enough students to fill the classes. The University is told it must fund the emphasis from its own budget.

But lack of new programs and lack of vitality in some existing ones, as well as moving from one S-curve to another, *requires* that the organization reallocate resources. Failure in these areas should not be laid on the doorstep of those who fund the institution. The organization has not mastered the art of "migrating across the discontinuity chasms."

The external environment has grown more complex in the last decade. The push for quality, accountability, and productivity is great. Meeting these demands is a constant battle. The faculty grows tired; it works hard.

In some areas, like many universities, it fails. Recruiting and retaining minority students is almost impossible (a fact true throughout the UW System). They do not come and they do not stay. System and individual campus response is to move higher on the "Minority Student" S-curve. More and more monies are used to "solve" the problem with few, if any, results. Perhaps our campus or some campus in UW System needs to move to a new S-Curve. What are the merits of establishing one campus in UW System as UW–Howard? This would be a high-quality campus, oriented and directed at stemming the alarming decline in the number of minorities in the UW System.

The structure of the organization, its human resources management, and the control system remain traditional. They have changed little in the last decade. As yet the organization is unable to become a meritocracy. Faculty recruitment has become more rigorous. There are probably more good young faculty on campus than good senior faculty. This creates its own tensions and is interesting to observe. Many good young faculty will arrive on campus in a brief number of years. Will they experience disillusionment similar to what was experienced by the large influx of faculty in the 1960s?

The University is a Defender organization, not a strong Defender, but it has moved from being a Reactor into planning and attending to its environment. The question of whether state systems of higher education can allow individual campuses to be strong Defenders or Analyzers is an important effectiveness issue. Until legislators are familiar with and are convinced of the merit of empowerment and intrapreneurship the answer will probably be "no." Thus, the organization is relatively tight; it has some looseness in the Faculty Development Program where empowerment is strongest. Power has moved (the Faculty Development Program notwithstanding) back to those in legitimate positions.

At the state level, it feels as if UW System is striving for a common culture systemwide—homogenized UW System campuses just like homogenized milk. Some decisions are inexplicable. In fiscally tight times the Regents receive a recommendation for one doctoral nursing program; the Regents fund two. In fiscally tight times UW System Administration embraces an idea of the governor for a Veterinary school—$40 million! But it still was not fully funded. The decisions defy the logic of dynamic networks as a new organizational form (Miles & Snow, 1986). But they fit a culture of "bigger is better."

THE INTRAPRENEURIAL CHANGES

Some changes involve what does not change. On-line registration/records work well even as student enrollments rise. Where would we be without it? It continues to impress students and their parents, especially if they have visited or been enrolled elsewhere.

The Calendar maintains itself. The new semester system has proved efficient and in its own way effective. There have been no major changes to alter it. However, the Calendar to this day has its detractors. "We have no final examination week," "Fourteen weeks is too short," "Some three-week courses cannot be taught with quality." Much of this grumbling can be understood as opposition to the old and new Chancellor. The Calendar is a visible target; it can be attacked. For some faculty the good old days are dead. There are always faculty who like to rattle their swords.

The data show that not many students make use (as was hoped) of seven-week courses. In general, as we have stated, many faculty themselves have not yet explored the power of the teaching "options" open to them. This lack of fuller use of the Calendar may be due to a failure by the organization to adopt and put in place better and different technologies of communication and decision-making which would support a more innovative curriculum. The organization has been unable to communicate to the Academic Deans, Department Chairs, and faculty the support for and the importance of new course offerings in new time modules. As a result, a culture and climate supporting such work never developed. The institution reverted to its "default position," that is, maintaining a relatively traditional curriculum.

Another reason for a lack of student use of scheduling opportunities is that the institution may have failed in development of different and effective technologies of communication and decision-making here as well. The options available to the students were not made clear. Today, with the capabilities of artificial intelligence and what can be done with computers, it would be possible to provide better and clearer information to students as they consider which courses to take and when to take them. Without this information and assistance, students stick mostly with courses taught in traditional time periods.

Of course, even with better communication and decision-making technology it is possible that innovative course offerings still would not have had a market. The *value* of such course offerings may simply be low in the eyes of the consumers.

Opposition to empowerment has been both overt and less visible. The Steward Chancellor is a strong manager; little new empowerment has been born under his tenure. More overtly, the faculty themselves have fought over who shall be empowered. Several years ago the Faculty Senate proposed sweeping committee reorganization within the University. In this proposal, the Senate would have taken control of Faculty Development. Committee reorganization failed. This clash of faculty cultures, between the "pols" and the Druids, resulted in continued empowerment for the Faculty Development Board (expert power). This conflict is a reminder of how hard it is to change culture, to really change how organizational members perceive, feel, and think through problems. Basic assumptions about reality are hard to compromise.

A valuable lesson is learned throughout the years. Maintaining intrapreneurial change never gets simple and never gets easier. It can get different. The University is an organization, trying to establish, even after a decade, new assumptions about its reality. The changes which came from the intrapreneurship (Calendar, Faculty Development) must be protected from established faculty, administrators, and from well-meaning new faculty who were not at the University at the time of change; the new people sacrificed nothing. Constant vigilance is required; empowerment is tiring.

Faculty want to live most in the realm of ideas, students, research, and writing. To maintain what they have gained requires that they live also in the realm of politics. So far enough of them have been interested in this to keep the Druid forest intact. Will it always be that way?

Faculty Development and its culture (perhaps because of its culture) has done well. Many facutly (about 70 percent) have participated in the program since its inception. It has been successful beyond anyone's expectations. It continues to allow faculty to exercise great power over what they want to be and to introduce new ideas into the organization. Those willing to do the work and participate have the opportunity to be heard.

It is an astonishing fact that neither political nor legitimate power in the University has made inroads in the Development Program during the fourteen years since its inception. The Deans who could attend meetings rarely do so. Our best guess would be that both sides see in Faculty Developent a symbol or vision of what academia is to be. Perhaps they see in its expert decision-making and its mission a vision of that which they wish they could be but cannot. The program has not been left alone because of the legitimate or political power of the Board's leaders. They are not strong enough for this.

Faculty Development has provided the organization with an unexpected success. The old guard is retiring. For the first time since the 1960s or early 1970s, new faculty in sizeable numbers are being recruited. And why do they come? Well, the University is no longer UW–Zero. But it also has Faculty Development. What started as a way to serve the faculty already at the University has become a prime recruitment and retention device. Faculty stay in part because of Faculty Development.

UW–Oshkosh had dreamed of a really innovative curriculum and a faculty broken free from the traditional academic time cycle. The dream, although only partially realized, is powerful. A subculture was established which allowed Faculty Development and expert decision-making to thrive. The institution became more knowledge-driven. Faculty development allowed knowledge to be the end as well as the means (Clark, 1987). The intrapreneurial action also forced and resulted in new and different people as administrators, loosening and dissolving the organization's ties to its past.

In summary, all major changes of the intrapreneurial era of 1974–1977 remain. Self-determination for both students and faculty is more possible than before. These core structures and beliefs have not been tampered with. But intrapreneurship and creative uses of the Calendar are in hibernation—deeply asleep. The question is whether anyone will come forth to awaken them and whether they have been asleep so long that they have turned to dust—dead. The intrapreneurs had sought " . . . to create the conditions of professional inspiration and self-regulation" (Clark, 1987, p. 275). Whether these conditions will be recaptured and felt to their fullest, we do not know.

References

Ashby, E. (1966). *Technology and the academics: An essay on universities and the scientific revolution*. New York: St. Martin's Press.

Bennis, W. (1975). The sociology of institutions, or Who sank the yellow submarine? Eleven ways to avoid major mistakes in taking over a university campus and making great changes. In J. V. Baldridge & T. E. Deal (Eds.), *Managing change in educational organizations* (pp. 328–340). Berkeley, CA: McCutchan Publishing Corporation.

Bennis, W., & Nanus, B. (1985). *Leaders: The strategies for taking charge*. New York: Harper & Row.

Betz, F. (1987). *Managing technology: Competing through new ventures, innovation, and corporate research*. Englewood Cliffs, NJ: Prentice-Hall.

Birnbaum, R. (1976). *University of Wisconsin–Oshkosh grant proposal*. (Available from the National Association of College and University Business Officers, One Dupont Circle, Suite 500, Washington, DC 20036).

Blackburn, R. T. (1977). *The Oshkosh calendar plan and its effectiveness*. Ann Arbor, MI: Higher Education Associates.

Block, P. (1987). *The empowered manager*. San Francisco: Jossey-Bass.

Bloom, A. (1987). *The closing of the American mind*. New York: Simon and Schuster.

Bowen, H. R. (1982). *The state of the nation and the agenda for higher education*. San Francisco: Jossey-Bass.

Boyer, E. L. (1987). *College: The undergraduate experience in America.* New York: Harper & Row.

Carnegie Commission on Higher Education. (1975). *More than survival: Prospects for higher education in a period of uncertainty.* San Francisco: Jossey-Bass.

Carnegie Council on Policy Studies in Higher Education. (1980). *Three thousand futures: The next twenty years for higher education.* San Francisco: Jossey-Bass.

Clark, B. R. (1975). The organizational saga in higher education. In J. V. Baldridge & T. E. Deal (Eds.), *Managing change in educational organizations* (pp. 98–107). Berkeley, CA: McCutchan Publishing Corp.

Clark, B. R. (1987). *The academic life: Small worlds, different worlds.* Lawrenceville, NJ: Princeton University Press.

Clifford, D. K., Jr., & Cavanagh, R. E. (1985). *The winning performance: How America's high-growth midsize companies succeed.* New York: Bantam Books.

Cohen, M. D., & March, J. G. (1974). *Leadership and ambiguity: The American college president.* New York: McGraw-Hill.

Davis, S. M. (1985). Culture is not just an internal affair. In R. H. Kilmann, M. J. Saxton, & R. Serpa (Eds.). *Gaining control of the corporate culture* (pp. 137–147). San Francisco: Jossey-Bass.

Deal, T. E. (1985). Cultural change: Opportunity, silent killer, or metamorphosis? In R. H. Kilmann, M. J. Saxton, & R. Serpa (Eds.), *Gaining control of the corporate culture* (pp. 292–331). San Francisco: Jossey-Bass.

Deal, T. E., & Kennedy, A. A. (1982). *Corporate cultures.* Reading, MA: Addison-Wesley.

Dickson, P. R., & Giglierano, J. J. (1986, July). Missing the boat and sinking the boat: A conceptual model of entrepreneurial risk. *Journal of Marketing, 50,* 58–70.

Dressel, P. L. (1987). Mission, organization, and leadership. *Journal of Higher Education, 58,* 101–109.

Drucker, P. F. (1973). Managing the public service institution. *The Public Interest, 33*(3), 43–60.

Drucker, P. F. (1985a). *Innovation and entrepreneurship: Practices and Principles.* New York: Harper & Row.

Drucker, P. F. (1985b). *The changing world of the executive.* New York: Time Books.

Drucker, P. F. (1988). The coming of the new organization, *Harvard Business Review,* January–February, 45–53.

Foster, R. (1986). *Innovation: The attackers advantage.* New York: Summit Books.

Gee, E. A., & Tyler, C. (1976). *Managing innovation.* New York: Wiley & Sons.

Hefferlin, L. J. B. (1969). *Dynamics of Academic Reform.* San Francisco: Jossey-Bass.

Jellema, W. (1986). The legacy of Rip van Winkle. In D. W. Steeples (Ed.), *Institutional revival: Case histories* (pp. 5–14). San Francisco: Jossey-Bass.

Kanter, R. M. (1972). *Commitment and community: Communes and utopias in sociological perspective.* Cambridge, MA: Harvard University Press.

Kanter, R. M. (1979). Changing the shape of work: Reform in academe. *Current Issues in Higher Education, 1,* 3–9.

Kanter, R. M. (1983a). *The change masters.* New York: Simon & Schuster, Inc.

Kanter, R. M. (1983b). Power. In D. W. Organ (Ed.), *The applied psychology of work behavior: A book of readings* (rev. ed.) (pp. 258–295). Plano, Texas: Business Publications, Inc.

Kaplan, R. (1987, May–June). Entrepreneurship reconsidered: The antimanagement bias. *Harvard Business Review,* pp. 84–89.

Keller, G. (1983). *Academic strategy: The management revolution in American Higher Education.* Baltimore, MD: The Johns Hopkins University Press.

Kiam, V. (1986). *Going for it!: How to succeed as an entrepreneur.* New York: William Morrow and Co., Inc.

Kilmann, R. H., Saxton, M. J., & Serpa, R. (1985). Conclusion: Why culture is not just a fad. In R. J. Kilmann, M. J. Saxton, & R. Serpa (Eds.), *Gaining control of the corporate culture* (pp. 421–433). San Francisco: Jossey-Bass.

Kuhn, T. S. (1970). *The structure of scientific revolution* (2nd ed.). Chicago: University of Chicago Press.

Labovitz, G. H. (1987, July 6). Keeping your internal customers satisfied. *The Wall Street Journal,* p. 12.

Leavitt, H. J. (1987). *Corporate pathfinders.* New York: Penguin Books.

Levine, C. (1979, Spring). Signpost: Hard time ahead. *University of Maryland Magazine, 7,* 19.

Lindquist, J. (1978). *Strategies for change.* Berkeley, CA: Pacific Soundings Press.

Louis, M. L. (1985). Sourcing workplace cultures: Why, when, and how. In R. H. Kilmann, M. J. Saxton, & R. Serpa (Eds.), *Gain-

ing control of the corporate culture (pp. 126–136). San Francisco: Jossey-Bass.

McMillen, L. (1987, April 15). Faculty-development programs seen often marginal to important campus needs. *Chronicle of Higher Education,* pp. 15–16.

Markus, M. L. (1984). *Systems in organizations.* Marshfield, MA: Pitman Publishing.

Miles, R. E., & Snow, C. C. (1978). *Organizational strategy, structure, and process.* New York: McGraw-Hill.

Miles, R. E., & Snow, C. C. (1984). Designing strategic human resources systems. *Organization Dynamics, 13,* 36–52.

Miles, R. E., & Snow, C. C. (1986). Organizations: New concepts for new forms. *California Management Review, 28* (3), 62–73.

Miller, W. F. (1988). The creative management of intellectual institutions. In R. E. Kunn (Ed.), *Handbook for creative and innovative managers* (pp. 577–586). New York: McGraw-Hill.

Mueller, R. K. (1987, April). Corporate networking. *Success,* pp. 50–52.

Naisbitt, J. (1984). *Megatrends: Ten new directions transforming our lives.* New York: Warner Books.

Naisbitt, J., & Aburdene, P. (1985). *Re-inventing the corporation.* New York: Warner Books.

Nayak, P. R., & Ketteringham, J. M. (1986). *Break-Throughs.* New York: Rawson Associates.

Peters, T., & Austin, N. (1985). *A passion for excellence: The leadership difference.* New York: Random House.

Peters, T., & Waterman, R. H. Jr. (1982). *In search of excellence.* New York: Harper & Row.

Peterson, H. L. (1978). A political analysis of organizational change: A case study of the University of Wisconsin–Oshkosh (Doctoral dissertation, University of Wisconsin–Madison, 1976). *Dissertation Abstracts International, 38,* 5284A.

Pinchot, G. III. (1985). *Intrapreneuring.* New York: Harper & Row.

Quinn, J. B. (1985a, June). Large scale innovation: Managing chaos. *Tuck Today,* pp. 2–7.

Quinn, J. B. (1985b, May-June). Managing innovation: Controlled chaos. *Harvard Business Review,* pp. 73–84.

Ramamurti, R. (1986). Public entrepreneurs: Who they are and how they operate. *California Management Review, 28*(3), 142–158.

Reich, R. B. (1987, May-June). Entrepreneurship reconsidered: The team as hero. *Harvard Business Review,* pp. 77–83.

Riley, P. (1983). A structurationist account of political culture. *Administrative Science Quarterly, 28,* 414–437.

Rutherford, W. (1978). *The Druids and their heritage.* New York: Gordon & Cremonesi.

Sagen, B. H., & Harcleroad, F. F. (1970). The developing state colleges and universities: Innovation or imitation? *North Central Association Quarterly, 44*(4), 335–351.

Sapienza, A. M. (1985). Believing is seeing: How culture influences the decisions top managers make. In R. H. Kilmann, M. J. Saxton, & R. Serpa (Eds.), *Gaining control of the corporate culture* (pp. 66–83). San Francisco: Jossey-Bass.

Sathe, V. (1985). How to decipher and change corporate culture. In R. H. Kilmann, M. J. Saxton, & R. Serpa (Eds.), *Gaining control of the corporate culture* (pp. 230–261). San Francisco: Jossey-Bass.

Schein, E. H. (1985a). *Organizational culture and leadership.* San Francisco: Jossey-Bass.

Schein, E. H. (1985b). How culture forms, develops and changes. In R. H. Kilmann, M. J. Saxton, & R. Serpa (Eds.), *Gaining control of the corporate culture* (pp. 17–43). San Francisco: Jossey-Bass.

Seib, K. (1984, January 25). How the laws of acadynamics work to prevent change. *Chronicle of Higher Education,* p. 72.

Smircich, L. (1983). Concepts of culture and organizational analysis. *Administrative Science Quarterly, 28,* 339–358.

Wahlquist, J. T., & Thornton, J. W. (1964). *State colleges and universities.* Washington, DC: The Center for Applied Research in Education, Inc.

Waterman, R. H. Jr. (1987). *The renewal factor.* New York: Bantam Books.

Wheelen, T. L., & Hunger, J. D. (1984). *Strategic management.* Reading, MA: Addison-Wesley.

Wood, C. (1977). *Working notes on Calendar.* Unpublished manuscript.

Wriston, H. M. (1959). *Academic procession: Reflections of a college president.* New York: Columbia University Press.

Yardley, J. (1987, July 5). Closing colleges is a political tussle. *The Milwaukee Journal,* p. 7 J.

Index

About the Authors

JAMES E. GUETHS is Administrative Vice President for the Wisconsin National Life Insurance Company responsible for Data Processing, Communications Technology, Computer Systems, Office Systems and Technology, Personnel and Staff Development. He received a B.A. degree from Ripon College in Physics and Mathematics, an M.S. degree (1963), and a Ph.D. (1966) in Physics from the University of Connecticut. He began teaching at the University of Wisconsin–Oshkosh in 1966 being promoted to a Professor in Physics. He served as Chairperson of the Physics and Astronomy Department at the University of Wisconsin–Oshkosh from 1969 to 1972 and as Director of a university-wide program for individualized, competency-based curricula in a variety of fields from 1973 to 1975. From 1975 to 1983 he was Assistant Vice Chancellor for Academic Systems. Dr. Gueths played a leadership role in the formation of the Richard W. Koehn Institute for Information Systems and Automation at the University and was its director. He has numerous professional presentations and publications. He also maintains an interest in the use of technology, leadership, and intrapreneurship within both private and public organizations.

BARON PERLMAN is a Rosebush Professor in the Department of Psychology at the University of Wisconsin–Oshkosh. He received his B.A. degree from Lawrence University in 1968 and his M.A. degree (1969) and Ph.D. (1974) in Clinical Psychology from Michigan State University. Since 1975 he has been a faculty member in the Department of Psychology at the University of Wisconsin–Oshkosh. He served as Graduate Coordinator of the Department's MS Psychology program from 1975 to 1983. Dr. Perlman served on the University's Faculty Development Board from 1976 to 1986, the last three years as its chairperson. Dr. Perlman is a member of numerous professional organizations and has presented and published extensively in areas of the management of mental health systems. He is presently interested and involved in research which studies intrapreneurship and innovation in institutions of higher education and other public institutions. He is also co-authoring a textbook titled, *Organizational Entrepreneurship: A Strategic Management Perspective*.

DONALD A. WEBER received a B.S. degree in Education from the University of Wisconsin–Milwaukee in 1967 and a Master's Degree in Education in 1970 from Kent State University. He served as an Assistant Director of Student Financial Aid at Kent State University from 1968 to 1970, and as Associate Director of Student Financial Aid at the University of Wisconsin–Oshkosh from 1970 to 1979. Since 1979 he has been Director of the Office of Grants at the University of Wisconsin–Oshkosh and has been the Vice Chancellor's representative to the Faculty Development Board. Mr. Weber is a member of the National Council of University Research Administrators.